JOHN

Chapters 11—21

J. Vernon McGee

THOMAS NELSON
Since 1798

NASHVILLE   DALLAS   MEXICO CITY   RIO DE JANEIRO

Published in Nashville, Tennessee, by Thomas Nelson, Inc.

Scripture quotations are from the KING JAMES VERSION of the Bible.

Library of Congress Cataloging-in-Publication Data

McGee, J. Vernon (John Vernon), 1904–1988
    [Thru the Bible with J. Vernon McGee]
    Thru the Bible commentary series / J. Vernon McGee.
       p.   cm.
    Reprint. Originally published: Thru the Bible with J. Vernon McGee. 1975.
    Includes bibliographical references.
    ISBN 0-7852-1042-3 (TR)
    ISBN 0-7852-1102-0 (NRM)
    1. Bible—Commentaries. I. Title.
BS491.2.M37   1991
220.7'7—dc20   90–41340
ISBN: 978-0-7852-0685-9   CIP

Printed in the United States
25 26 27 28 29 EPAC 14 13 12 11 10

CONTENTS

JOHN—Chapters 11—21

PREFACE

The radio broadcasts of the Thru the Bible Radio five-year program were transcribed, edited, and published first in single-volume paperbacks to accommodate the radio audience.

There has been a minimal amount of further editing for this publication. Therefore, these messages are not the word-for-word recording of the taped messages which went out over the air. The changes were necessary to accommodate a reading audience rather than a listening audience.

These are popular messages, prepared originally for a radio audience. They should not be considered a commentary on the entire Bible in any sense of that term. These messages are devoid of any attempt to present a theological or technical commentary on the Bible. Behind these messages is a great deal of research and study in order to interpret the Bible from a popular rather than from a scholarly (and too-often boring) viewpoint.

We have definitely and deliberately attempted "to put the cookies on the bottom shelf so that the kiddies could get them."

The fact that these messages have been translated into many languages for radio broadcasting and have been received with enthusiasm reveals the need for a simple teaching of the whole Bible for the masses of the world.

I am indebted to many people and to many sources for bringing this volume into existence. I should express my especial thanks to my secretary, Gertrude Cutler, who supervised the editorial work; to Dr. Elliott R. Cole, my associate, who handled all the detailed work with the publishers; and finally, to my wife Ruth for tenaciously encouraging me from the beginning to put my notes and messages into printed form.

Solomon wrote, ". . . of making many books there is no end; and much study is a weariness of the flesh" (Eccl. 12:12). On a sea of books that flood the marketplace, we launch this series of THRU THE BIBLE with the hope that it might draw many to the one Book, *The Bible.*

J. VERNON MCGEE

The Gospel According to

JOHN

INTRODUCTION

It is generally assumed that the Gospel of John is easy to understand. Often you hear the cliché, "The Gospel of John is the *simple* Gospel." And the simplicity of the language has deceived a great many folk. It is written in monosyllabic and disyllabic words. Let me lift out a couple of verses to illustrate. Notice how simple these words are: "He came unto his own, and his own received him not. But as many as received him, to them gave he power to become the sons of God, even to them that believe on his name" (John 1:11–12).

We have no problem with the words themselves, but actually, we're dealing here with the most profound Gospel. Take an expression like this: "ye in me, and I in you" which appears in John 14:20. Seven words—one conjunction, two prepositions, and four pronouns—and you could ask any child in the fourth grade the meaning of any one of those words and he could give you a definition. But you put them together—"ye in me, and I in you"—and neither the most profound theologian nor the greatest philosopher has ever been able to probe the depths of their meaning. "Ye in me" we know means salvation; "and I in you" means sanctification, but beyond that none of us can go very far. We think, sometimes, because we know the meaning of words that we know what is being said. The words are simple, but the meaning is deep.

Jerome said of John's Gospel, "John excels in the depths of divine mysteries." And no truer statement was ever made. Dr. A. T. Pierson put it like this, "It touches the heart of Christ."

Though it is assumed that John is the simple Gospel, it's not always assumed that the apostle John is the author of it. The Baur-Tübingen School in Germany years ago began an attack upon the Gospel of John. And this has been a place where the liberal has really had a field day. I took a course in seminary (even in my day) on the authorship of the Gospel of John. The professor finally concluded the course by saying he thought John was the author. A wag in the class remarked, "Well, I believed John wrote it before I started the class and I believe it now; so I just wasted a semester!" Let me assure you that we are not going to waste time here relative to the authorship of this Gospel other than to mention two statements that make it quite obvious that John is the writer of it.

One of the reasons it was felt that John might not be the writer was because Papias (I've quoted him now for each of the Gospels) was thought to have never mentioned the authorship of John. But Professor Tischendorf, the German who found the Codex Sinaiticus, which is probably our best manuscript of the Old Testament, down in Saint Catherine's Monastery in the Sinaitic peninsula, was working in the Vatican library when he came upon an old manuscript that has a quotation from Papias in which it was made clear that John was the author of this Gospel. I personally wouldn't want any better authority than that. Also, Clement of Alexandria, who lived about A.D. 200, makes the statement that John was persuaded by friends and also moved by the Spirit of God to write a spiritual Gospel. And I believe that the Gospel of John is that spiritual Gospel. In my mind there's not a shadow of doubt that John is the author.

However, the more significant question is: Why did John write his Gospel? It was the last one written, probably close to A.D. 100. All the other apostles were dead, the writers of the New Testament were all gone, and he alone was left. In an attempt to answer this question we find again a diversity of theories. There are those who say that it was written to meet the first heresy of the church which was Gnosticism. The Gnostics believed that Jesus was God but not man at all, that the apostles only thought they saw Him, but actually did not. And Irenaeus expressly makes the statement that the purpose of John was to confute the Gnostic Cerinthus. But Tholuck makes it very clear that this is not a polemic Gospel at all, and he is not attempting to meet that issue. Also, there are those who say that it is a supplement to what the others had written, that he merely added other material. But Hase answers that by saying, "This Gospel is no mere patchwork to fill up a vacant space."

You see, these theories do not give an adequate answer to account for all the peculiar facts that are in this Gospel which a true explanation must do. And, in my judgment, the only satisfactory explanation is that John wrote at the request of the church which already had three Gospels (Matthew, Mark, and Luke were being circulated) and wanted something more spiritual and deep, something that would enable them to grow. That's exactly what Augustine, the great saint of the early church, said:

> In the four Gospels, or rather in the four books of the one Gospel, the Apostle St. John not undeservedly with reference to his spiritual understanding compared to an eagle, has lifted higher, and far more sublimely than the other three, his proclamation, and in lifting it up he has wished our hearts also to be lifted (Gregory, *Key to the Gospels*, pp. 285–286).

That is the purpose of the Gospel of John. That is the reason that he wrote it.

Accordingly, therefore, when we come to the Gospel of John, we find that he does not take us to Bethlehem. We will never grow spiritually by singing "O Little Town of Bethlehem" umpteen times at Christmas. John won't take us to Bethlehem because he wants you and me to grow as believers. John takes us down the silent corridors of eternity, through the vast emptiness of space, to a beginning that is not a beginning at all. "In the beginning was the Word" (John 1:1). Some say that this world came into being three billion years ago. I think they're pikers. I think it has been around a lot longer than that. What do you think God has been doing in eternity past, twiddling His thumbs? May I say to you, He had a great deal to do in the past, and He has eternity behind Him. So when you read, "In the beginning," go as far back as your little mind can go into eternity past, put down your peg—and Jesus Christ comes out of eternity to meet you. "In the beginning was [not is] the Word, and the Word was with God, and the Word was God" (John 1:1). Then come on down many more billions of years. "All things were made by him; and without him was not any thing made that was made" (John 1:3). Then John, in the fourteenth verse, takes another step: "And the Word was made flesh, and dwelt among us" (John 1:14).

The Greek philosophers and the Greek mind for which Luke wrote would stop right there and say, "We're through with you. We can't follow you." But John was not writing for them, and he goes even further. "No man hath seen God at any time; the only begotten Son, which is in the bosom of the Father, he hath declared him" (John 1:18). "Declared him" is *exegeted* Him, led Him out in the open where man can see Him and come to know Him. The Man who had no origin is the Son who comes out of eternity.

Luke, who was a medical doctor, looked at Him under a "microscope." Though John's method is altogether different, he comes to the same conclusion as did Luke. You could never call John's method scientific. The Christian who has come to a knowledge of Christ and faith in Him doesn't need to have the virgin birth gone over again; he already believes that. Therefore, when he comes to the Gospel of John, he finds sheer delight and joy unspeakable as he reads and studies it.

Unfortunately, though, he thinks the unbeliever ought to have it also. And you'll find it is used in personal work more than any other Gospel. After all, doesn't the average Christian consider it the simple Gospel? Is it simple? It's profound. It's for believers. It enables them to grow.

When I was a pastor in Pasadena, I had a doctor friend who, because of his position, was able to get together students at Cal Tech for a Bible class. Do you know what he taught? You're right, the Gospel of John. He told me, "You know, I really shook that bunch of boys with the first chapter." I met him several weeks after that and asked him how the class was getting on. "Oh," he said, "they quit coming." Well, after all, they had been in a school where you pour things into a test tube, where you look at things under a microscope. I said, "Why didn't you take the Gospel of Luke?" "Because," he said, "I wanted to give them the simple Gospel." Well, he didn't. John is not simple; it's profound. It is for believers.

Also there was a seminary professor in this area not long ago who was asked to teach the Bible to a group of businessmen at a noon luncheon. Guess what book he taught. You're right! He said, "They don't know very much, so I'll give them the Gospel of John." I wish he'd given them the Gospel of Mark. That's the Gospel of action, the Gospel of power, the Gospel for the strong man. But he gave them the Gospel of John.

The Gospel of John is for those who already believe. When you come to chapters thirteen through seventeen you can write a sign over it, *For Believers Only*, and you could put under that, *All Others Stay Out*. I don't think that section was ever meant for an unbeliever. Jesus took His own into the Upper Room and revealed to them things that enabled them to grow. And no other Gospel writer gives us that. Why? Because they're the evangelists who are presenting Christ as the Savior of the world. Somebody asks, "But doesn't John do that?" Yes, he does, but he is primarily writing for the growth of believers.

John gives more about the resurrected Christ than does any other Gospel writer; in fact, more than all the others put together. Paul said that, though we have known Christ after the flesh, we don't know Him that way anymore. Rather, we know Him as the resurrected Christ. For this reason John attempts to give the appearances of Jesus after His resurrection, and he mentions seven of them.

The first was one of the most dramatic as He appeared to Mary Magdalene there in the garden. The second was to the disciples in the Upper Room, Thomas being absent. The third appearance was again to the disciples in the Upper Room with Thomas present (these three appearances are recorded in ch. 20). Then we see Him appearing by the Sea of Galilee. Several disciples were out fishing. He called to them from the shore, "Do you have any fish?" (see John 21:5).

He is going to ask you that some day, and He's going to ask me. Have you been doing any fishing recently? Well, you catch them only the way he tells you. You have to fish by His instructions.

And then He prepared breakfast for them. I wish I had been there for that outdoor breakfast. That was a real cookout. And friend, He still wants to feed you in the morning—also during the day and in the evening—with spiritual food. Then He commissioned Simon Peter: "Simon, do you love Me?" (see John 21:15–17). Jesus did not say that you have to be a graduate of a seminary to be able to serve Him. He asked, "Do you love Me?" That's the one condition. Don't misunderstand me. If you love Him you will want training to prepare you for the ministry He has for you, but He wants to know that you love Him. The reason multitudes of folk are not serving Him today is that they do not love Him. And then Peter was told that he was to be a martyr; but John, no, he will live on in order to write this Gospel, three epistles, and the Book of Revelation. There are the seven appearances that John records, and all of them are for believers; they minister to us today.

At the time of the birth of Christ there was a great expectation throughout the heathen world. That was a strange thing.

Suetonius relates that "an ancient and definite expectation had spread throughout the East, that a ruler of the world would, at about that time, arise in Judaea." Tacitus makes a similar statement. Schlegel mentions that Buddhist missionaries traveling to China met Chinese sages going to seek the Messiah about 33 A.D. (*Life of Vespasian*, c. iv.).

There was an expectation throughout the world at that time that He might come. And it was out of the mysterious East that the wise men came to Jerusalem, "Saying, Where is he that is born King of the Jews? . . ." (Matt. 2:2).

The marvel is that this Gospel of John, so definitely designed to meet the need of believers, is also designed for the oriental mind as is no other. Whom do I mean by Orientals? The Egyptians, the Babylonians, the Persians, the uncounted millions in India and in China. Even to this good day we know so little about that area of the world. What about Tibet or Outer Mongolia? It is still the mysterious East. We do know this: there is fabulous wealth there, and right next to it is abject poverty. Out of this land of mystery came the wise men. They were bringing gifts—gold, frankincense, and myrrh for Him. There are a lot of questions to be answered there. Out of that land of mystery they came. That oriental splendor that we've heard so much about reveals unbelievable wealth, and it is still there—ornate palaces, gaudy grandeur, priceless gems. It has so entranced the West that when Columbus started out for this country (we give him credit for discovering America, but he wasn't looking for our continent), he was trying to find a new route to the East in order to bring back something of the wealth that was there.

However, by the side of that wealth there is extreme poverty of the basest sort, dire destitution, millions living in squalor and misery. Their worldly goods consist of the rags they have on their backs. One hundred million will die of starvation in this next decade, we're told. You may ask, "Well, why don't we send food for them?" There's not enough to go around. Our decision is which hundred million will starve? Will it be these or those? But the thing that arrests us is that the poor were crying for help, and the wealthy had found no solution to the problems of life. The Orient gave freest reign to human desires. Although they had this freedom, there was no satisfaction. They've had the great pagan religions—Buddhism, Shintoism, Hinduism, Confucianism, and Mohammedanism. Yet out of that area, with all that they had, their wise men came asking, ". . . Where is he that is born King of the Jews? for we have seen his star in the east, and are come to worship him" (Matt. 2:2). They needed salvation. They had none; no religion ever gave that to them. And this is the reason people in the mysterious East have reveled in the Gospel of John as no others have. It is a mind today that will revel in the Gospel of John. The Lord Jesus can meet the need of this type of mind, as John reveals.

Out of heaven's glory He came, that One who was before any beginning that we can envision. "And the Word was made flesh" and walked down here among men. The Orient had religion. After all, Israel belonged to that area of the world. The Orient had all kinds of religion. They had temples—ornate, hideous, with degrading rituals. They had cults of the occult. And John tells us that the first public act of the Lord Jesus was to go into the temple of that day and cleanse it. By this He is telling them something, these people who worshiped in their degrading temples, that God is holy. If you're going to worship God you'll have to be cleansed; the temple will have to be cleansed; there can be no compromise with evil or wrong.

A religious ruler came to Jesus one night—John alone tells us this. Our Lord that night said to this religious ruler, who had everything and was religious to his fingertips, "You must be born again" (see John 3:3). He needed to have a new life and get rid of the old religion. Jesus said that He had not come to sew a patch on the old garment, but He came to give them the robe of righteousness that would enable them to stand before a holy God. This is what that area of the world needed.

Womanhood was degraded in the Orient. Our Lord ennobled womanhood because He came, born of a woman. He went to a wedding to answer the mockery that they'd made of marriage with the harems of the East. Christ went to a wedding and put His blessing upon it. Also Jesus sat down at a well and had a conversation with a woman of very questionable character. But she was a woman for whom He later died. The soul of a woman was as precious to Him as the soul of a man.

Christ fed the multitudes, followed the meal with a discourse on the Bread of Life, and then escaped because He did not want them to make Him king of their stomachs.

The oriental mind would understand Jesus' discourse on the Bread of Life. It is unfortunate that the managers of our supermarkets don't understand it—they think it's bread and beans on the shelf that's important, and He said it's not. A man in the Orient who hasn't bread and beans will understand that. I am afraid some of us miss it today.

The Lord Jesus said in this Gospel, "I am the light of the world; I am the bread of life; I am the way, the truth and the life." And the Orient was wretched and perishing in that day, as it is today. John says, "And many other signs truly did Jesus in the presence of his disciples, which are not written in this book: but these are written, that ye might believe that Jesus is the Christ, the Son of God; and that believing ye might have life through his name" (John 20:30–31). The thing that they needed above everything else was life. And, friend, this is what the whole world needs today—not religion, but life!

Now before we begin our study of this magnificent Gospel, let me call your attention to some striking features.

The first three Gospels are called the synoptic Gospels because they are written from the same viewpoint with a similar pattern. The fourth Gospel is different.

1. Matthew and Mark emphasize the miracles of Jesus, and Luke gives attention to the parables. John does neither.

2. The miracles in John are given as signs and were chosen with a great deal of discrimination in order to interpret certain great truths. (For example, the discourse on the Bread of Life follows the feeding of the five thousand.) There are eleven specific signs in the Gospel of John.

3. There are no parables in the fourth Gospel. The word *parable* does occur one time in John 10:6, but it is not the regular Greek word *parabolē* but *paroimia*. This word ought not to be translated "parable" at all. The story of the Good Shepherd is not a parable; it is a discourse.

John gives us a chronological order which is well to note. The fact of the matter is, if you will follow it along, it will give you a ladder on which you can fit the three-year ministry of Christ. (For example, in John 1:29, 35 he says, "The next day . . . , the next day.") He's giving not only a logical but also a chronological sequence in his Gospel. He also gives attention to places and cities—for example, "Bethabara beyond Jordan" (John 1:28); "Cana of Galilee" (John 2:1).

The deity of Christ is emphasized in this Gospel and is actually in the foreground. But the humanity of Christ is not lost sight of. Do you notice it is only John who tells about His trip through Samaria, and that He sat down at the well, and that He was weary with His journey? Can you think of anything more human than that? Well, I can think of one thing—Jesus wept. And it is John who tells us that, by the way.

The name *Jesus* is used almost entirely to the exclusion of *Christ* in this Gospel. That is strange because the emphasis is upon the deity of Christ, and you'd think that he would use the name *Christ*. Then why does he use the name *Jesus*? It is because God became a man.

There is a mighty movement in this Gospel, and it is stated in John 16:28. "I came forth from the Father, and am come into the world: again, I leave the world, and go to the Father." God became a man; this is the simple statement of the sublime fact.

OUTLINE

I. **Prologue—Incarnation, Chapter 1:1–18**
  A. Word Is God, Chapter 1:1–3
  B. Word Became Flesh, Chapter 1:14
  C. Word Revealed God, Chapter 1:18

II. **Introduction, Chapter 1:19–51**
  A. Witness of John the Baptist, Chapter 1:19–36
  B. Witness of Andrew, Chapter 1:37–42
  C. Witness of Philip, Chapter 1:43–46
  D. Witness of Nathanael, Chapter 1:47–51

III. **Witness of Works and Words, Chapters 2—12**
  A. Jesus at Marriage in Cana (First Work), Chapter 2:1–12
  B. Jesus Cleanses Temple During Passover in Jerusalem (First Word), Chapter 2:13–22
  C. Jesus Interviews Nicodemus in Jerusalem (Second Word), Chapter 2:23—3:36
  D. Jesus Interviews Woman at Well in Sychar (Third Word), Chapter 4:1–45
  E. Jesus Heals Nobleman's Son in Capernaum (Second Work), Chapter 4:46–54
  F. Jesus Heals Man at Pool of Bethesda (Third Work), Chapter 5
  G. Jesus Feeds Five Thousand on East of Sea of Galilee (Fourth Work and Word), Chapter 6
  H. Jesus Teaches at Feast of Tabernacles in Temple (Fifth Word), Chapter 7
  I. Jesus in Temple Forgives Woman Taken in Adultery (Sixth Word), Chapter 8
  J. Jesus Opens Eyes of Man Born Blind in Jerusalem (Fifth Work), Chapter 9
    1. Record of Miracle, Chapter 9:1–7
    2. Reaction to Miracle, Chapter 9:8–41

Another division of the Gospel of John:
LIGHT—John 1—12
LOVE—John 13—17
LIFE—John 18—21

CHAPTER 11

THEME: Jesus raises Lazarus from the dead in Bethany (sixth work)

JESUS RAISES LAZARUS FROM THE DEAD IN BETHANY (Sixth Work)

Let's pause for a moment to get the perspective of John. In the first ten chapters, Christ has revealed Himself in an ever widening circle. This began at the wedding of Cana where there were guests and also His disciples. We are told that His disciples believed on Him. At the Feast of Tabernacles and the Feast of Dedication, the whole nation was before Him. He presented Himself to the nation and He was rejected: His works were rejected in John 5:16; His words were rejected in John 8:58–59; and His Person was rejected in John 10:30–31.

This chapter is a kind of intermission. His public ministry is over and He retires into a private ministry. Centering Himself on individuals, He no longer is reaching out to the nation. The events of this chapter occur between the Feast of Dedication and the Passover which would be sometime between December and April.

The Gospel of John is like climbing up a mountain in that each chapter brings us a little higher than the preceding chapter. Remember that John has told us why he wrote this Gospel: "And many other signs truly did Jesus in the presence of his disciples, which are not written in this book: but these are written, that ye might believe that Jesus is the Christ, the Son of God; and that believing ye might have life through his name" (John 20:30–31). Going back to the very beginning: "In the beginning was the Word, and the Word was with God, and the Word was God" (John 1:1). "And the Word was made flesh, and dwelt among us" (John 1:14). While He walked among us in the flesh, this great thesis was sustained by miracle and parable and discourse.

Now the supreme question is: Can Jesus raise the dead? The big question in any religion concerns death. Death is a great mystery. And life is a great mystery, but life is practically meaningless if there is no resurrection of the dead. The question to ask of any religion is whether it has power over death.

Liberal theologians long ago threw out the miraculous. They contend that nothing miraculous belongs in the Bible—not because of any scholarly reason, but simply because they don't believe in the miraculous. Today there is a synthetic doctrine that goes something like this: "I believe in a religion of the here and now, not the hereafter. I don't go for pie in the sky by and by. I want a meat and potatoes religion, one that is practical, not theoretical." Now that is something I want also. And in addition, I want a hope.

Although we are given many benefits right here and now, the greatest of all benefits is eternal life in Christ Jesus. It is very practical to ask the question: "Will the dead be raised?" Life is so brief. Life's little day compared to eternity is infinitesimal. Recently I conducted the funeral of a very wonderful Christian man—and there sat his wife and mother. Certainly they considered the resurrection very practical. When you stand at a graveside, if you have no hope, you are whistling in the dark and singing in the rain and crying the blues.

I notice that in cults and religions of the day there are all kinds of chicanery and racketeering, but nobody is in the business of raising the dead. Although some of them have claimed they can raise the dead, they never produce the body, the corpus delicti. When Jesus healed the sick, it was the body that was healed. When Jesus raised the dead, it was the body that was raised. Many religions promise much for this life, but nothing for the hereafter. That is like taking someone for an airplane ride without knowing how to land the plane. The great hope of the Christian faith is the resurrection of the dead!

The Gospels tell us three incidents of Jesus raising the dead. There was the twelve-year-old girl who had just died. She was a juvenile. There was a young man, whose body was being carried to the cemetery. Then there was Lazarus, possibly a senior citizen, who had been dead four days and had been buried. They were all raised, from every age group.

Allow me to be technical and state that these people were raised from the dead but were not resurrected. Rather, it was a restoration to life. Resurrection is this: ". . . It is sown in corruption; it is raised in incorruption: it is sown in dishonour; it is raised in glory: it is sown in weakness; it is raised in power: It is sown a natural body; it is raised a spiritual body . . ." (1 Cor. 15:42–44). These people were raised from the dead, but none of them were given glorified bodies. They all faced death again. Christ is the firstfruits of them that sleep. His is the only true resurrection—". . . Christ the firstfruits; afterward they that are Christ's at his coming" (1 Cor. 15:23).

While our Lord used different methods to perform His miracles of healing, His method of raising the dead was always the same. He called to them and spoke to them as if they heard Him. Do you know why He did that? Because they heard Him! I think that when He returns with a shout, every one of us will hear his own name because He will call us back from the dead.

Now let's get into the chapter.

> **Now a certain man was sick, named Lazarus, of Bethany, the town of Mary and her sister Martha.**
>
> **(It was that Mary which anointed the Lord with ointment, and wiped his feet with her hair, whose brother Lazarus was sick.) [John 11:1–2].**

Note that Bethany is the town of Mary. This was written about A.D. 90 and by that time people knew about Mary who had anointed the feet of Jesus with spikenard. The fragrance of the box that she broke still fills this world. Jesus said that her act of devotion would be remembered wherever the gospel was preached. I am of the opinion that many a humble person is breaking an alabaster box of ointment and will have more recognition in heaven than many well-known Christian leaders who receive much publicity down here.

It was the home of Martha. Our Lord had visited there before. Martha had been cumbered and frustrated with her preparations for dinner. Jesus had told her that to sit at His feet and learn of Him is better than being too busy with service.

It was the town of Mary and the home of Martha. There are different gifts. Some women are given a marvelous gift in the home. Talk about women's liberation! I know of no one who is the big boss more than a wife and a mother in her home. She can hustle you out of the kitchen, make you stay out of the refrigerator, and tell you to move when she wants to vacuum. She is in charge of the kitchen and of the whole house. This is the calling of many Christian women. There are others who have an outside ministry. They teach Bible classes and child evangelism classes, and work in the church. Remember, friend, the woman who serves in her home can be serving the Lord and the woman who serves outside her home can be serving the Lord. The Holy Spirit bestows gifts for many types of ministries.

> **Therefore his sisters sent unto him, saying, Lord, behold, he whom thou lovest is sick [John 11:3].**

These are humble folk, and they make no request, no demand of Him. They tell Jesus the problem and let Him decide what to do. So often in prayers I hear the people demanding that the Lord heal the sick. When did God become a Western Union boy? When did He become a waiter to wait upon us or a redcap boy to carry our suitcase? He doesn't do things that way. Mary and Martha knew their Lord! "Lord, behold, he whom thou lovest is sick."

"He whom thou lovest." Lazarus is loved by the Savior. Paul said, "He loved me" (see Gal. 2:20). John called himself the disciple whom Jesus loved. Peter declared that Jesus loves us. And by the way, He loves you and He loves me. Anyone who is a child of God is one whom Jesus loves.

> **When Jesus heard that, he said, This sickness is not unto death, but for the glory of God, that the Son of God might be glorified thereby [John 11:4].**

Jesus, you see, was not in Bethany at the time, and a message was sent to Him.

Some people say that a Christian should never be sick. Is sickness in the will of God? I wish Lazarus were here to tell you about that. Sickness is not a sign that God does not love you. "For all this I considered in my heart even to declare all this, that the righteous, and the wise, and their works, are in the hand of God: no man knoweth either love or hatred by all that is before them" (Eccl. 9:1). In other words, you cannot tell by the circumstances of a man whether God loves him or not. You have no right to judge. "Therefore judge nothing before the time, until the Lord come, who both will bring to light the hidden things of darkness, and will make manifest the counsels of the hearts . . ." (1 Cor. 4:5). Jesus loved Lazarus when he was sick. Not only that, Jesus will let Lazarus die—but He still loves him.

Now Jesus loved Martha, and her sister, and Lazarus.

When he had heard therefore that he was sick, he abode two days still in the same place where he was [John 11:5–6].

He loves you when you are sick, He loves you when you are well, He loves you all the time. You can't keep Him from loving you. You may ask why He lets certain difficulties happen to you. I don't know the reason, but I do know He loves you. He loves you whether or not you are a Christian. You can't keep Him from loving you. You can't stop the sun from shining, but you can get out of the sunshine. And you can put up an umbrella to keep the love of God from shining upon your life.

Because He loves us, we are to come with boldness to present our problems to Him. Boldness means freedom of speech, opening your heart to Him. Boldness does not mean that your requests can be demands of God. Trouble tests our faith and puts us on our knees. Moses cried unto the Lord repeatedly when problems arose in the wilderness wanderings. Hezekiah took the threatening letter from the Assyrians and presented it to the Lord. The disciples of John the Baptist came to the Lord with the heartbreaking news when John was beheaded. My friend, it is down in the valley, even in the valley of the shadow of death, that we must learn to trust Him. He teaches us patience, teaches us that we can rest in Him, teaches us that He works all things well. We need to look beyond the tears, the sorrows, and the trials of life, and see that God has a purpose in everything that happens.

"This sickness is not unto death, but for the glory of God." Jesus permits this to happen because God will get the glory in it. We need to learn that *we* are not the center of the universe—nor is our home, our church, our town. The headquarters of everything are in heaven, and everything is running for *His* glory. Nothing will come into our lives without His permission, and if He permits it, it is going to be for His glory.

I do want you to notice that the Lord loved Martha. Sometimes we are very hard on Martha, very critical of her. The commentaries haven't been kind to her. She was cumbered with much serving and she hadn't learned the best thing, but that did not keep our Lord from loving her.

Does it seem cruel that Jesus let Lazarus die? No, there is a message here for us. The Lord Jesus was not motivated by sentiment, but He was subject to the Father's will. Human sentiment would urge Him to go to Bethany immediately. But He deliberately let Lazarus die. Friend, sometimes He allows our loved ones to die. We need to recognize that He has a reason, and His ways are perfect. Jesus never moves by sentiment. That is what spoils people and that is how parents spoil their children. He is motivated by love, and that love is for the good of the individual and for the glory of God.

> **Then after that saith he to his disciples, Let us go into Judaea again.**
>
> **His disciples say unto him, Master, the Jews of late sought to stone thee; and goest thou thither again? [John 11:7–8].**

Don't miss that word *again*. He had been there and had been forced to withdraw. Now He returns and takes His disciples with Him into the danger zone.

Jesus answered, Are there not twelve hours in the day? If any man walk in the day, he stumbleth not, because he seeth the light of this world.

But if a man walk in the night, he stumbleth, because there is no light in him [John 11:9-10].

There are twelve hours in the day, and you can't change that. Because the Father has given the Son a work to do, nothing can stop Him. There is a great principle here. God has given to each man a lifework. You can't extend that for one day any more than you can keep the sun from going down in the afternoon. But, thank God, you are absolutely invulnerable until your work is done. Nobody, not even Satan, can thwart God's purpose in your life if you are following Him. To fail to follow Him is dangerous. Then one is in darkness because He is the Light of the World. You can go into the danger zone with Him, and you won't be touched. You will finish your work. But if you stay out in the darkness, if you walk in the darkness, you will stumble. There has been death in Bethany. If there is to be light in that time of darkness, Jesus must go there. He is the Light of the World.

These things said he: and after that he saith unto them, Our friend Lazarus sleepeth; but I go, that I may awake him out of sleep.

Then said his disciples, Lord, if he sleep, he shall do well.

Howbeit Jesus spake of his death: but they thought that he had spoken of taking of rest in sleep.

Then said Jesus unto them plainly, Lazarus is dead.

And I am glad for your sakes that I was not there, to the intent ye may believe; nevertheless let us go unto him [John 11:11-15].

The disciples did not understand what Jesus meant when He said that Lazarus was sleeping. Because many people today do not understand it either, we find people who talk about soul-sleep. Friend, sleep is for the body, never for the soul. This is true of both sleep in this life and the sleep of death. Death means separation. The body of the believer sleeps in the grave, but the spirit goes to be with Christ. For the believer, to be absent from the body is to be present with the Lord (see 2 Cor. 5:8). Jesus is called the firstfruits of them that sleep. Does this mean that Jesus is sleeping somewhere today? Absolutely not. He is in His glorified body. The believer goes immediately to be with the Lord, but the body sleeps until the day of resurrection when the body will be raised.

Death, for the believer, is a sleep for his body. Are you afraid of sleep? You shouldn't be. Sleep is a relief from labor. It is the rest that comes for renewal and preparation for the new day that is coming. There is nothing quite as beautiful as the word sleep when it is used for the death of a believer. The body is put to sleep, to be awakened by our Lord. He is the only One who has the alarm clock. He is the only One who can raise the dead. One day He will come and we shall awaken in our new bodies.

The Greek word for resurrection is *anastasis* which means "a standing up." C. S. Lewis, that brilliant Oxford don, ridiculing those who hold that resurrection is spiritual rather than physical, asked, "If it is the spirit that stands up, what position does it take?" There's a question to work over! No, resurrection means a standing up, and it always refers to the body. The soul never dies, nor does the soul ever sleep.

Death is a reality, an awful reality of the body. But, remember, the resurrection is also reality. You see, man leaves off at death. Even in the hospital, there is a finality about death. Doctors will work and work over a patient. Then when he dies, they all stop working. When death comes, they are through. Science is helpless in the presence of death. Where man must leave off, Jesus begins. Resurrection is also reality.

A man in Pasadena told me, "When you die, you die just like a dog." I answered, "Don't you wish that were true? But," I said, "if it's not true (and I think that bothers you a little), you're in trouble, aren't you?" He turned away because he didn't want to talk about that. People are afraid of death.

Mrs. McGee and I were in Wichita, Kansas, for a Bible conference, staying at a large motel there. We had dinner before the evening service and the bar room was loud with the "happy hour." When we returned in the evening, word had arrived that the airplane carrying the football team had gone down. The coach and the first line of football players all had been killed. "Happy hour" was like a morgue then. They were silent, without hope.

> **Then said Thomas, which is called Didymus, unto his fellow-disciples, Let us also go, that we may die with him [John 11:16].**

Thomas is a gloom-caster, isn't he? He thinks he is going to die along with Jesus. But, thank God, he was willing to do just that. I believe Thomas meant it, too, just as Simon Peter meant it.

> **Then when Jesus came, he found that he had lain in the grave four days already.**
>
> **Now Bethany was nigh unto Jerusalem, about fifteen furlongs off:**
>
> **And many of the Jews came to Martha and Mary, to comfort them concerning their brother [John 11:17–19].**

Bethany is about two miles from the Golden Gate at Jerusalem. Many of the Jews walked from Jerusalem to Bethany to be with Martha and Mary. Apparently they were a prominent family in Bethany and were well known in Jerusalem.

> **Then Martha, as soon as she heard that Jesus was coming, went and met him: but Mary sat still in the house.**
>
> **Then said Martha unto Jesus, Lord, if thou hadst been here, my brother had not died.**

**But I know, that even now, whatsoever thou wilt ask of
God, God will give it thee [John 11:20–22].**

Martha seems always to be the aggressive type. She is the woman of
action. She reveals a wonderful faith but also an impatience and a lack
of bending to the will of God. By contrast, Mary is willing to sit at
home. She has learned to sit at Jesus' feet.

We can see now that Martha should have been sitting at Jesus' feet
a little more. She says, "I know that if You will ask God." Martha,
don't you realize that *He* is God? He is God, manifest in the flesh. He
has been in your home, sat at your table and has eaten your biscuits,
but you didn't realize that He was God, did you? Oh, my friend, how
we need to spend time at His feet. How we need to listen.

Jesus saith unto her, Thy brother shall rise again.

**Martha saith unto him, I know that he shall rise again
in the resurrection at the last day.**

**Jesus said unto her, I am the resurrection, and the life:
he that believeth in me, though he were dead, yet shall
he live:**

**And whosoever liveth and believeth in me shall never
die. Believest thou this? [John 11:23–26].**

Martha believed in a resurrection. But listen, it makes less demand
upon faith to believe that in a future day we shall receive glorified
bodies than it does to rest now on the assurance that they that wait
upon the Lord shall renew their strength. It is easier to believe that the
Lord is coming and the dead will be raised than it is to believe that
tomorrow I can live for God. It is so easy to comfort people who are
mourning and say, "Well, you'll see your loved ones someday." That
doesn't take much faith. It takes a lot of faith to say, "I have just lost
my loved one but I am comforted with the assurance that God is with
me and He does all things well." You see, although Martha knew from
the Old Testament that there would be a resurrection from the dead,
she didn't believe that Jesus could help her now.

Jesus says to her, "Martha, don't you know that I *am* the resurrection and the life?" If we have Jesus, we have life. "He that believeth in me, though he were dead" is referring to spiritual death. Though a person is spiritually dead, "yet shall he live." Then He looks into the future and says that the one who has trusted Him shall never die. Life begins at the moment a person accepts the Savior. Whosoever lives and believes in Jesus will never die because Jesus has already died for him. That is, he will never die a penal death for his sins. He will never be separated from God. Then Jesus asks the question: "Believest thou this?"

> **She saith unto him, Yea, Lord: I believe that thou art the Christ, the Son of God, which should come into the world [John 11:27].**

Martha gives the same confession that Peter gave. She understands that He is the Messiah.

> **And when she had so said, she went her way, and called Mary her sister secretly, saying, The Master is come, and calleth for thee.**
>
> **As soon as she heard that, she arose quickly and came unto him.**
>
> **Now Jesus was not yet come into the town, but was in that place where Martha met him.**
>
> **The Jews then which were with her in the house, and comforted her, when they saw Mary, that she rose up hastily and went out, followed her, saying, She goeth unto the grave to weep there [John 11:28–31].**

Although Martha had told Mary secretly, God will overrule this—the whole crowd will be at the cemetery. They don't know that she is going out to meet Jesus.

> **Then when Mary was come where Jesus was, and saw
> him, she fell down at his feet, saying unto him, Lord, if
> thou hadst been here, my brother had not died [John
> 11:32].**

She was saying along with Martha that if Jesus had been there, her
brother would not have died. This is why Jesus will say later on that it
was expedient, it was better, for Him to go away. This incident makes
it obvious why it was expedient. As long as He was here in the flesh,
He was limited geographically. If He were in your town, He couldn't
be in my town. If Jesus had not gone away, He could not have sent the
Comforter, the Holy Spirit. But now that the Holy Spirit has come, He
is everywhere. He indwells every believer today. So the Holy Spirit can
be where I am, where you are, and on the other side of the world si-
multaneously. "Nevertheless I tell you the truth; It is expedient for you
that I go away: for if I go not away, the Comforter will not come unto
you; but if I depart, I will send him unto you" [John 16:7].

> **When Jesus therefore saw her weeping, and the Jews
> also weeping which came with her, he groaned in the
> spirit, and was troubled,**
>
> **And said, Where have ye laid him? They said unto him,
> Lord, come and see.**
>
> **Jesus wept [John 11:33–35].**

If you want to know how God feels about the death of your loved ones,
look at this. He groaned in the spirit and was troubled. Death is a
frightful thing. And you can be sure that He enters into sympathy
with you.

His sympathy was for the living. He knew what He was going to do
for the dead. "Jesus wept." While John's Gospel is written to show us
the deity of Christ, here Jesus is shown in all His humanness. He even
asked where Lazarus was laid because He was so human. And here we
can see the way God feels at a funeral today. He mingles His tears with
ours. He groans within Himself. I get a little impatient with Christians

who say one must not cry at a funeral, but one must be a brave Christian. Death is not pretty; it is a terrible thing. Jesus *wept!*

> **Then said the Jews, Behold how he loved him!**
>
> **And some of them said, Could not this man, which opened the eyes of the blind, have caused that even this man should not have died? [John 11:36–37].**

The Jews missed the point here. He wept, not because He loved Lazarus—He was not weeping for the dead—He wept for those who were living.

You notice that the Jews go back to the incident of healing the blind man. That obviously made a great impression on them.

> **Jesus therefore again groaning in himself cometh to the grave. It was a cave, and a stone lay upon it.**
>
> **Jesus said, Take ye away the stone. Martha, the sister of him that was dead, saith unto him, Lord, by this time he stinketh: for he hath been dead four days.**
>
> **Jesus saith unto her, Said I not unto thee, that, if thou wouldest believe, thou shouldest see the glory of God? [John 11:38–40].**

The subject of death is skirted by people today. The undertakers try in every way to make death seem like a pleasant episode. But let us face it very frankly, we can't cover up death by embalming and painting up the face, dressing the body in a good suit of clothes, then placing it in a pretty coffin surrounded by flowers. Although this is done to help soften the shock, death is an awful thing.

Martha said that he had been buried for four days already and his body would stink; it would be decaying. Someone may think that sounds crude. So is death crude. It is awful. This case is certainly going to require a miracle.

Then they took away the stone from the place where the dead was laid. And Jesus lifted up his eyes, and said, Father, I thank thee that thou hast heard me.

And I knew that thou hearest me always: but because of the people which stand by I said it, that they may believe that thou has sent me [John 11:41-42].

Remember that this whole incident is for the glory of God. Jesus prays audibly to let the people know that what He is going to do is the will of the Father so that the Father will get the glory. He voices His prayer for the benefit of those who are present.

And when he thus had spoken, he cried with a loud voice, Lazarus, come forth.

And he that was dead came forth, bound hand and foot with graveclothes: and his face was bound about with a napkin. Jesus saith unto them, Loose him, and let him go [John 11:43-44].

I want to mention here that I think there were multitudes raised from the dead by Jesus Christ. I think there were multitudes who were healed, hundreds of blind people who received their sight. The Gospels record only a few instances for us.

Notice that for Lazarus, life was restored to the old body. He came out still wrapped in all the graveclothes. When our Lord rose from the dead, He left all the graveclothes in place just as they had been wrapped around His body, including the napkin which had been wrapped around His head. He came right out of them. Why? Because He came out in a glorified body. They didn't need to roll away the stone for Jesus to come out. It was rolled away so the people on the outside could look in and see that the tomb was empty. His glorified body could leave the sealed grave and it could also enter a room with all the doors locked.

There is a beautiful picture of salvation in this. We were dead in trespasses and sins, dead to God, and are now made alive to God in

Christ Jesus. But, friend, each of us is being held back by those grave-clothes. Paul could say, ". . . For what I would, that do I not; but what I hate, that do I. . . . O wretched man that I am! . . ." (Rom. 7:15, 24). This was not an unsaved man talking; this was a believer. Jesus wants us to be free from those graveclothes. He says, "Loose him, and let him go."

> **Then many of the Jews which came to Mary, and had seen the things which Jesus did, believed on him.**
>
> **But some of them went their ways to the Pharisees, and told them what things Jesus had done [John 11:45–46].**

These men cannot ignore this miracle.

It may surprise you to learn that this is the end of the public minis-try of Jesus when you see that we are only near the halfway mark in the Gospel of John. His public ministry began when John the Baptist marked Him out as the Lamb of God. It concluded when He raised Lazarus from the dead. John, you see, spent almost as much time on the last forty-eight hours before His death as he did on the first thirty-two years, eleven months, three weeks, and five days of His life. As a matter of fact, this is the pattern shared by all the Gospel writers. They placed the emphasis on the last eight days. There are eighty-nine chapters in the four Gospels. Four of these chapters cover the first thirty years of the life of Jesus and eighty-five chapters the last three years of His life. Of those eighty-five chapters, twenty-seven deal with the last eight days of His life. So about one-third of the Gospel records deal with the last few days and place the emphasis on the death and resurrection of Jesus Christ.

Friend, it is a misrepresentation of the gospel if the death and res-urrection of Jesus Christ are not preeminent. In fact, that comprises the gospel (see 1 Cor. 15:1–4). The Gospel writers did what Paul also did later on. He says, "For I determined not to know any thing among you, save Jesus Christ, and him crucified" (1 Cor. 2:2).

You would think that this crowning miracle would have turned these skeptics to Jesus, but it did not. Our Lord had said previously, you remember, ". . . If they hear not Moses and the prophets, neither will they be persuaded, though one rose from the dead" (Luke 16:31). That is the reason that God does not rend the heavens and come down in spectacular display. That is the reason God does not go about performing miracles today. After the church leaves the earth, during the Great Tribulation period, and into the Millennium, there will be a period of great miracles, but even that will not convince people. Today we are asked in a quiet way to put our trust in Him even though the mob and the majority turn from Him. People complain that the crowd isn't going after Jesus. Friend, it never did! He died, He was buried, He rose again from the dead, and that is the gospel. We don't need a miracle. The problem is not in the lack of evidence. The problem is the unbelief of man.

Then gathered the chief priests and the Pharisees a council, and said, What do we? for this man doeth many miracles [John 11:47].

You can see here that the problem for these bloodhounds of hate was not a lack of evidence. His enemies said, "He doeth many miracles." They couldn't deny His miracles.

This is a diabolical group. The chief priests at this time were largely Sadducees who were the "liberals" in that they did not accept miracles or the supernatural—which included resurrection. The Pharisees were the religious conservatives and the political rightists of that day. The two parties were absolutely opposed to each other in every way; yet here they join together in their hatred of Jesus Christ and in their determination to put Him to death. You might label this the first ecumenical movement. If men can get rid of Jesus Christ, they will join with even those of opposing views in their antagonism toward Him. This is the trend of the hour. The majority is attempting to get rid of Christ as He is revealed in the Word of God. It is the minority that accepts Jesus Christ as He is.

If we let him thus alone, all men will believe on him: and the Romans shall come and take away both our place and nation [John 11:48].

They feared there would be a mass turning to Jesus Christ which would bring a revolution. This would provide an occasion for Rome to pounce on them. They moved from a basis of fear. Fear is the motivation which keeps a great many people away from Jesus today. Even in our churches Christians lack the intestinal fortitude to stand on their two feet for the truth of Scripture and for men who teach it as the Word of God.

> And one of them, named Caiaphas, being the high priest that same year, said unto them, Ye know nothing at all,
>
> Nor consider that it is expedient for us, that one man should die for the people, and that the whole nation perish not.
>
> And this spake he not of himself: but being high priest that year, he prophesied that Jesus should die for that nation;
>
> And not for that nation only, but that also he should gather together in one the children of God that were scattered abroad [John 11:49–52].

They begin to rationalize and say that Jesus should die rather than the nation die at the hand of Rome. It is interesting to note that although they did succeed in putting Jesus to death, in spite of this, the nation perished when Titus destroyed it in A.D. 70.

We find a strange thing here: Caiaphas' accurate prediction because he was high priest that year! Caiaphas was a scheming politician, and later we will meet his father-in-law Annas, who was also a mean rascal and the power behind the throne. That Caiaphas had the gift of prophecy should not fool us. Like Balaam in the Old Testament, this rascal could utter a true prophecy.

> Then from that day forth they took counsel together for to put him to death.

Jesus therefore walked no more openly among the Jews;
but went thence unto a country near to the wilderness,
into a city called Ephraim, and there continued with his
disciples [John 11:53–54].

This is the beginning of the end, friend. They are openly trying to put
Jesus to death and are openly hostile. We don't know exactly where
the city Ephraim is. It was probably out in rather wild country.

And the Jews' passover was nigh at hand: and many
went out of the country up to Jerusalem before the passover, to purify themselves.

Then sought they for Jesus, and spake among themselves, as they stood in the temple, What think ye, that
he will not come to the feast?

Now both the chief priests and the Pharisees had given a
commandment, that, if any man knew where he were,
he should shew it, that they might take him [John
11:55–57].

The crowds come to Jerusalem to purify themselves before the Passover. As they go through this endless ritual and rub shoulders with
each other, there are differences of opinion and talk about Jesus. They
wonder whether Jesus will come to the feast this year. They know the
Sanhedrin is really after Him. You see, if they will not believe Moses,
they will not believe even though one rose from the dead.

At this point John's Gospel has reached the breaking point. We are
approaching the last week of the earthly life of the Lord Jesus Christ.

CHAPTER 12

THEME: Witness of Jew and Gentile to Jesus; Jesus comes to Bethany for supper; Jesus comes to Jerusalem—tearful entry; Jesus comes to Greeks; Jesus comes to His hour; Jesus comes to end of His public ministry

WITNESS OF JEW AND GENTILE TO JESUS

As we come to this twelfth chapter, we are going with Jesus to make a visit to a home, the home of Lazarus, Mary, and Martha of Bethany. In this Gospel of John, He opened His public ministry at a wedding in Cana of Galilee; He closes His public ministry by a visit to this home. Our Lord put an emphasis upon the home, the Christian home, the godly home. Marriage has the blessing of God upon it. So we come now to this lovely picture.

JESUS COMES TO BETHANY FOR SUPPER

Then Jesus six days before the passover came to Bethany, where Lazarus was which had been dead, whom he raised from the dead.

There they made him a supper; and Martha served: but Lazarus was one of them that sat at the table with him.

Then took Mary a pound of ointment of spikenard, very costly, and anointed the feet of Jesus, and wiped his feet with her hair: and the house was filled with the odour of the ointment [John 12:1–3].

In Jerusalem they were plotting and planning His death but, here in Bethany, His friends plan a dinner party for Him. Right in the shadow of the Cross, those who loved Him made Him a dinner. We want to study the whole picture of this lovely dinner.

Lazarus, the man who has been raised from the dead was in fellowship with Christ. Jesus had said, "I am the resurrection, and the life: he that believeth in me, though he were dead, yet shall he live" (John 11:25). This was true of Lazarus in a physical sense. He had been raised from the dead. It is true of you and of me in a spiritual sense. We were dead in trespasses and sins. We had no knowledge of Him nor did we have any fellowship with Him. So for us He said, "And whosoever liveth and believeth in me shall never die" (John 11:26).

What a picture we have here! There is Lazarus alive from the dead and in fellowship with Christ. Then we see Mary sitting at Jesus' feet, growing in grace and in the knowledge of Christ. Then, thirdly, we see Martha serving, putting on a meal. That is her gift and she is exercising it. These are the three essentials in the church today: new life in Christ, worship and adoration, and service. This home at Bethany should be a picture of your church and mine.

All this is in the home where Jesus is with His own. As you know, the church began in the home. It may end in the home. Many of our churches are turning away from God and the things of God. They are no longer places of delightful fellowship and blessing. So perhaps the church will return to homes where true fellowship with Christ will be found.

Then we notice the devotion and adoration, the unutterable attachment and deep affection of this woman, Mary. She anointed the feet of Jesus with costly spikenard and wiped them with her hair. Some people think this is the same story as the harlot who washed Jesus' feet. I think you will have trouble with Mary someday if you think that. She is an altogether different person. The only thing that is the same in both cases is that the hair was used to wipe His feet. The odor of the ointment filled the house. Delightful!

Then saith one of his disciples, Judas Iscariot, Simon's son, which should betray him,

Why was not this ointment sold for three hundred pence, and given to the poor?

This he said, not that he cared for the poor; but because he was a thief, and had the bag, and bare what was put therein [John 12:4–6].

Judas Iscariot is revealing his true nature. He is the treasurer of the group. He doesn't care for the poor; he cares for himself—he is a thief. He was taking some money out on the sly. He wants Mary's money given to the poor so he can handle it and take out his percentage.

May I say to you today, the real test of a Christian, the hard-coin test, is the way he handles his finances. The real test of a church or a Christian organization is the way it handles its finances. Is the money used for the cause for which it was given, or is it shifted and used in some other way?

Three hundred pence was the annual wage of a laboring man of that day. Because the spikenard was too costly for Mary to use on herself, she poured it all out on Jesus. Friend, if we would learn to sit at His feet, we would give more to Him, too. Mary had saved this precious ointment in an alabaster box. It came out of India, where the herbs grow high in the Himalayas, and was very expensive. Do you know why she had bought it and saved it? So that when she died it could be used on her body! Now she pours it all out on Him. This is absolute affection, adoration, and attachment to His Person. The odor of that ointment filled the house, and it still fills the world today.

Then said Jesus, Let her alone: against the day of my burying hath she kept this.

For the poor always ye have with you; but me ye have not always [John 12:7–8].

This is a really remarkable incident. The Lord here reveals that this woman anoints Him to let Him know that she enters into His death. She senses that He is to die for the sins of the world and she anoints Him ahead of time. Matthew recorded that Jesus said that wherever the gospel would be preached, this incident would be told. This is true. Even today the wonderful fragrance of this thing that she did fills the world.

What a contrast we find here between her and Judas Iscariot. Here is where light and darkness are coming together. Judas is the darkness and Mary is the light.

There is an application for us today. Jesus says that the poor are always with us and that He will not always be with us. He is not contradicting His statement that He is with us always, that He will never leave us nor forsake us. What He is saying here is that we can always be of service to the poor—but they are always with us—but that our service should not be a substitute for sitting at His feet. There comes a day when it is too late to absorb all He has for us. I get letters saying, "Dr. McGee, I never had Bible teaching; if only I had had Bible teaching when I was young." My friend, learn about Him now. Do not substitute activity for sitting at His feet.

> **Much people of the Jews therefore knew that he was there: and they came not for Jesus' sake only, but that they might see Lazarus also, whom he had raised from the dead.**

> **But the chief priests consulted that they might put Lazarus also to death;**

> **Because that by reason of him many of the Jews went away, and believed on Jesus [John 12:9-11].**

These people are curiosity seekers. The chief priests wanted to get Lazarus out of the way. I personally believe that the people came out of curiosity to see Lazarus rather than to see Jesus and that the faith described here is much like the faith exhibited when Jesus first came up to Jerusalem. Remember that they believed on Him, but He would not commit Himself to them. It was a belief based on curiosity.

JESUS COMES TO JERUSALEM—TEARFUL ENTRY

On the next day much people that were come to the feast, when they heard that Jesus was coming to Jerusalem [John 12:12].

Notice how John gears this One who came out of eternity into the calendar of the world. It is the time before the Feast of the Passover, and the crowd is expectant. Remember that in Matthew's record Jesus was born and sought by the wise men who called Him the King of the Jews. Now, at the end of His ministry, He is again presented as the King of the Jews.

Took branches of palm trees, and went forth to meet him, and cried, Hosanna: Blessed is the King of Israel that cometh in the name of the Lord.

And Jesus, when he had found a young ass, sat thereon; as it is written,

Fear not, daughter of Sion: behold, thy King cometh, sitting on an ass's colt [John 12:13–15].

This is the public offer of Himself as their King and the rulers, of course, reject it. He is no longer mixing among the people and teaching them. That had already ceased. This is now an act which He performs as a fulfillment of prophecy. He is offering Himself to the nation. This is not really a *triumphal* entry. He came in through the sheep gate, quietly, during His public ministry. All through His public ministry, He tended to withdraw from the crowds. Now, when His public ministry is over, He does the most public thing He has ever done. He steps out publicly and presents Himself.

He does this to fulfill prophecy. "As it is written." He rides into Jerusalem to fulfill the Word of God and to fulfill the will of God. John gives us a very brief account of this entry of Jesus, but he does say that if fulfills the prophecy of Zechariah 9:9: "Rejoice greatly, O daughter of Zion; shout, O daughter of Jerusalem: behold, thy King cometh unto thee: he is just, and having salvation; lowly, and riding upon an ass, and upon a colt the foal of an ass." Jesus presents Himself publicly to Jerusalem as the Messiah. They acclaim Him with "Hosanna: Blessed is the King of Israel that cometh in the name of the Lord." What will Israel do with their King? They will crucify Him.

> **These things understood not his disciples at the first: but when Jesus was glorified, then remembered they that these things were written of him, and that they had done these things unto him [John 12:16].**

John is writing this many years later, and he admits that he didn't understand what Jesus was doing that day. Probably he asked James and Peter and Andrew, and they didn't understand either. Mary was the only one who had entered into His death. The others didn't understand until after His death and resurrection. "When Jesus was glorified, then remembered they that these things were written of him."

> **The people therefore that was with him when he called Lazarus out of his grave, and raised him from the dead, bare record.**
>
> **For this cause the people also met him, for that they heard that he had done this miracle.**
>
> **The Pharisees therefore said among themselves, Perceive ye how ye prevail nothing? behold, the world is gone after him [John 12:17–19].**

Here is a situation loaded with dynamite. The crowd is enthusiastic because of His miracle; their interest is centered on Lazarus and not on the person of Christ. The Pharisees are out to kill Him. Jerusalem is crowded with people for the feast.

Obviously, Jesus Christ could have had the crown without first going to the Cross. However, if He had gone directly to the crown, if He were the ruler today, you and I would never have been saved. He had to go to the Cross to save you and me. Although this was a brief moment of triumph before His death, it was not His triumphal entry. In the future when He enters as Lord of lords and King of kings, that will be His triumphal entry.

My favorite painting of the Crucifixion shows three empty crosses. The bodies of the crucified have been taken down from the crosses and lie in the tombs. In the background is a little donkey eating on a palm frond. What a message! The discarded palm branch and the Cross are the tokens of His so-called triumphal entry. Where is the crowd that cried, "Hosanna: Blessed is the King of Israel that cometh in the name of the Lord"? They may be the same crowd that on the next day shouted, "Crucify Him!" Now they are gone, and He is in the tomb. You see, He offered Himself to them publicly as their King, but He was rejected.

JESUS COMES TO GREEKS

And there were certain Greeks among them that came up to worship at the feast:

The same came therefore to Philip, which was of Bethsaida of Galilee, and desired him, saying, Sir, we would see Jesus.

Philip cometh and telleth Andrew: and again Andrew and Philip tell Jesus [John 12:20–22].

Apparently Jesus has gone into the temple. Since there is a court for the women and a court for the Gentiles, these Greeks cannot go in where Jesus is. Philip has a Greek name and may have spoken Greek, which is probably the reason they came to him. Philip is a modest and retiring fellow and he goes to Andrew for help. Together they bring the Greeks to Jesus.

And Jesus answered them, saying, The hour is come, that the Son of man should be glorified.

Verily, verily, I say unto you, Except a corn of wheat fall into the ground and die, it abideth alone: but if it die, it bringeth forth much fruit [John 12:23-24].

When our Lord says "verily," He is about to say something very important to hear. And when He says, "verily, verily," it is of supreme importance.

He that loveth his life shall lose it; and he that hateth his life in this world shall keep it unto life eternal [John 12:25].

"Jesus answered them"—I think "them" includes both the disciples and the Greeks. It seems that Jesus went out to speak to them. I do not believe He would refuse to come to anyone who was asking for Him.

The Greeks want to see Jesus because they had heard about Him, probably about His miracles, and especially His raising of Lazarus from the dead. Now He directs the attention of the Greeks to His Cross. He is in the shadow of the Cross. He tells them, "The hour is come." What hour? The hour of crisis for which He came out of eternity and toward which His entire life has moved. You remember that He had said to His mother early in His ministry, "mine hour is not yet come" (John 2:4). Now His hour is come. He is going to the Cross.

His conception of the Cross was far different from that held by the Roman populace. To them it was an instrument of infamy and disgrace and shame. It was the hangman's noose, the electric chair, and the gas chamber. He became obedient to death, even the death of the Cross. Why? "Christ hath redeemed us from the curse of the law, being made a curse for us: for it is written, Cursed is every one that hangeth on a tree" (Gal. 3:13). Then on the third day He was raised from the dead and crowned with glory and honor ". . . for the joy that was set before him [he] endured the cross, despising the shame, and is set down at the right hand of the throne of God" (Heb. 12:2). The glory of God is seen in that Cross. That is why He could say that the time had come for Him to be glorified. Friend, He was glorified when He died for you and me. He was glorified when He came forth from that tomb. Mercy and pardon and forgiveness are found at that Cross.

Then our Lord states a great principle using the physical analogy of a grain of wheat. Although a grain of wheat in the ground dies, it produces the blade, the ear, and the harvest. It must die to bring forth fruit. Many people think they have seen Jesus because they have read the Gospels and they have studied His life. They see the historical Jesus, but they have never seen Jesus until they comprehend His death and His resurrection. He died a redemptive death. He gave His life in death so that we might have life. You haven't seen Jesus until you have seen that He is the One who died for you on the Cross. He is the One who died for the sins of the world.

This seems a strange thing to be saying to the Greeks who had come to see Him. He is telling them that there is more than just seeing Him physically. The important thing for them to see is that He is going to die. He is going to be put into the ground. When that grain of wheat died, it produced life. He died, but He rose again. That is so important to see.

He goes on to explain a great axiom to the Greeks. There are two kinds of life and they are put in contrast here. There is what is known as the psychological life, the life of the psyche, life that enjoys the things of this world and finds satisfaction in the gratification of the senses. It is the kind of life that really whoops it up down here. "He that loveth his life" refers to this physical, natural life that we have. You can really live it up, drink it up, take drugs, paint the town red, but do you know what is going to happen? One day you are going to die. You'll lose it. I'm sorry, but you will lose it, friend.

I heard of a sensational preacher down in Texas who was asked to preach at the funeral of a rich man of the town who had been a church member but had broken every law of God and man and was living in sin and in drunkenness. This was in the oil section of Texas and a lot of rich people, the fast crowd, the jet set, came to the funeral. Now this preacher did something I wouldn't do, but maybe I should do it, although I never have done it. He preached a gospel message! Then he stepped down to the casket and he preached on what sin will do for an individual and that it will finally send a man to hell. I tell you, the folks were getting uneasy. Then when he invited them to view the remains, he said, "His life is past; he lived it up; he is through. He despised God and he turned his back on Jesus Christ." Then he looked at that crowd and said, "This is the way each one of you is going to end up unless you turn to Jesus Christ." Now, friend, that is making it very plain—maybe a little too plain.

We do need to tell it like it is. This is what our Lord says. "He that loveth his life shall lose it." That is, if you live it up down here, you'll lose it. Then our Lord makes a contrast. "He that hateth his life in this world shall keep it unto life eternal." This means that if you do not live for this world or for the things of this world, you keep your life unto life eternal. And eternal life comes from what? It comes through the death of that grain of wheat that fell onto the ground and rose again, the Lord Jesus Christ. That is the way you can save your life—the only way you can save it.

If any man serve me, let him follow me; and where I am, there shall also my servant be: if any man serve me, him will my Father honour [John 12:26].

He tells them to follow Him, and He is on His way to the Cross. He promises that where He is, His servants will also be. "If any man serve me, him will my Father honour."

JESUS COMES TO HIS HOUR

Now is my soul troubled; and what shall I say? Father, save me from this hour: but for this cause came I unto this hour [John 12:27].

There is a suffering that is connected with the Cross of Christ that you and I cannot comprehend. He didn't suffer at the hands of men only. That was bad enough, but He suffered beyond that. Your sin and my sin were put upon Him. He was ". . . a man of sorrows, and acquainted with grief . . ." (Isa. 53:3) there on the Cross. He bore the sin of the world, not His own sin. "Surely he hath borne our griefs, and carried our sorrows . . ." (Isa. 53:4). Our sin was put upon Him. He was made sin for us—not in some academic manner—He actually was made sin for us. "Yet it pleased the LORD to bruise him; he hath put him to grief . . . [He made] his soul an offering for sin" (Isa. 53:10). Although He was holy and undefiled and separate from sinners, He was made sin for you and for me. This involved a suffering that you and I cannot comprehend.

> But none of the ransomed ever knew
> How deep were the waters crossed;
> Or how dark was the night that the
>   Lord passed through
> Ere He found His sheep that was lost.
>   "The Ninety and Nine"
>   —Elizabeth C. Clephane

His soul stood in horror; He was aghast before that Cross. Yet He had come into the world for the purpose of going to the Cross and enduring the shame of it. Also there was glory in the Cross, friend. We ought to think more about it and thank Him more. Paul says, "But God forbid that I should glory, save in the cross of our Lord Jesus Christ, by whom the world is crucified unto me, and I unto the world" (Gal. 6:14).

Do you see how this ties in with the two preceding verses? Our Lord is facing the supreme sacrifice—shortly He will give His life as a ransom for the human family. And He has put this challenge to those who are following Him: "He that hateth his life in this world shall keep it unto life eternal. If any man serve me, let him follow me." You can tell where a person is going by the way that person is living. Someone may say, "I thought we are saved by faith—you always emphasize faith rather than works." That's right. I surely do. If you are going to be saved, you will have to put your trust in Him—". . . Believe on the Lord Jesus Christ, and thou shalt be saved . . ." (Acts 16:31). But I want to say that if you truly trust Him, it is going to change your life. If it doesn't change your life, then you aren't really trusting Him.

When I see a Christian who mortgages every dime he has just to own every gadget to live in luxury down here, I wonder how he can be waiting for the Lord to come, and hoping for it with real anticipation. "He that loveth his life shall lose it."

Notice also how this ties in with His saying, "Where I am, there shall also my servant be: if any man serve me, him will my Father honour." It is not a question of the Lord going with us, but of our being where the Lord is. One man said to me, "Well, you know, I'm a member of a liberal church, but I take the Lord with me." My friend, I have news for you. The Lord doesn't go to church there. The Lord is not going to go your way. You are to go where the Lord is.

Our salvation is not cheap. This "hour" is repulsive to our Lord. If it were possible, He would want the Father to spare Him from the horror of being made sin, although He knows this is the reason He came into the world. Then He says, "Father, glorify thy name."

Father, glorify thy name. Then came there a voice from heaven, saying, I have both glorified it, and will glorify it again [John 12:28].

His supreme desire is the glory of God. What a lesson that is for us! We tend to whimper and cry and complain and ask God why He lets unpleasant things happen to us. With Christ, we should learn to say, "Father, through this suffering and through this pain, glorify Thyself."

Heaven couldn't remain silent but had to respond. God answered audibly. Have you noticed that God spoke to Him from out of heaven on three occasions: at the beginning, midway, and at the end of His ministry? Have you noticed that all three occasions are related to the death of Christ? The first was at His baptism when He was identifying Himself with sinful humanity. The second time was at His transfiguration when Elijah, Moses, and the Lord Jesus were talking about His decease which He should accomplish in Jerusalem (see Luke 9:30–31). This third time, at the conclusion of His ministry, the Lord is talking about His death because His hour has come.

> **The people therefore, that stood by, and heard it, said that it thundered: others said, An angel spake to him.**
>
> **Jesus answered and said, This voice came not because of me, but for your sakes [John 12:29–30].**

Now which group was right? Neither was right. It wasn't an angel; it was the Father speaking to Him. One group did believe it was supernatural; they knew it was articulate. They knew about the ministry of angels in the Old Testament and understood that God's messages for man generally came through "the angel of the Lord." They did not, however, understand that "the angel of the Lord" was the preincarnate Christ. They did acknowledge that the voice from heaven brought a message from God.

The other group said it thundered. They gave it a natural explanation. That is the same reaction many people still have today. They say God's Word is full of errors and the miracles recorded can't be accurate. Because they don't believe in them, they say it just "thundered." Some folk who were attending a Bible class where they were listening to my tapes on Revelation were told by a liberal preacher that nobody could understand the Book of Revelation, that it didn't make sense. He revealed his own ignorance because the Book of Revelation is a very logical book and probably the most systematic book in the Bible. But, you see, to him it was thunder. It was just noise.

The Word of God says that His birth was supernatural. His life was filled with miracles, and His death was like a grain of wheat. He didn't stay in the ground, friend; He came up just like the grain of wheat. The liberal who said, "The bones of Jesus sleep somewhere beneath Syrian skies" has a problem on his hands. Where are the bones? Christ's resurrection was not spiritual but actual. It was His body that was raised—His bones just don't happen to be anywhere on earth. Yet, this is the same old gag that has been used down through the years, "it thundered." It is no mark of intelligence to say that. We need spiritual perception and appreciation to hear and to know and to see the Word of God. We need to recognize that the Spirit of God must enlighten us when we come to the Word of God.

> Now is the judgment of this world: now shall the prince of this world be cast out.
>
> And I, if I be lifted up from the earth, will draw all men unto me.
>
> This he said, signifying what death he should die [John 12:31–33].

Christ's death on the Cross was the judgment of the world and of the prince of this world. That is one of the things the Holy Spirit will bear witness to, according to John 16:7–11. We live in a world that is judged. He came to die a judgment death for the sins of the world. If the world will not accept this, the world is judged.

How is Satan, the prince of this world, cast out? I believe it is done gradually. When Christ died on the Cross, I am convinced that Satan did not understand what was happening. What he thought would be a defeat turned out to be a victory. He lost the battle at the Cross which is the reason the Lord can say that the prince of this world is cast out. Then in Revelation 12:10 we are told that Satan will be cast out of heaven, which is the second stage. Then in Revelation 20:3, he will be cast into the bottomless pit, and in Revelation 20:10, he will be cast into the lake of fire. That is the last stage of his defeat. At the Cross, his doom was sealed. The Cross marks the victory of Christ and the defeat of Satan.

Jesus puts the emphasis on His redemptive death. His death will draw all men unto Him. Those who believe will be saved. Those who reject Him will be lost.

Consider how important it is to lift up Jesus before men, to put the emphasis on His redemptive death. There are multitudes passing by the church today who are not hearing the Word. Think of the laborers, the students, the men in the uniform of our country, the white-collar group, the rich. They do not hear. Jesus, the crucified Lord, is not being lifted up in the churches today. Friend, the gospel needs to be preached, and the gospel is about a Christ who was crucified.

> **The people answered him, We have heard out of the law that Christ abideth for ever: and how sayest thou, The Son of man must be lifted up? who is this Son of man? [John 12:34].**

The crowd is really confused. They say, "When Christ comes, He will reign forever, and now You say that You are not abiding but are going to die." They just did not understand. What was wrong?

> **Then Jesus said unto them, Yet a little while is the light with you. Walk while ye have the light, lest darkness come upon you: for he that walketh in darkness knoweth not whither he goeth.**

> **While ye have light, believe in the light, that ye may be the children of light. These things spake Jesus, and departed, and did hide himself from them [John 12:35–36].**

Jesus now withdraws and this ends His public ministry. He will never appear publicly again until He comes to this earth to establish His Kingdom.

JESUS COMES TO THE END OF HIS PUBLIC MINISTRY

> **But though he had done so many miracles before them, yet they believed not on him:**

That the saying of Esaias the prophet might be fulfilled, which he spake, Lord, who hath believed our report? and to whom hath the arm of the Lord been revealed?

Therefore they could not believe, because that Esaias said again,

He hath blinded their eyes, and hardened their heart; that they should not see with their eyes, nor understand with their heart, and be converted, and I should heal them.

These things said Esaias, when he saw his glory, and spake of him [John 12:37–41].

Now we learn what was wrong. Although they were standing in the presence of the Light of the World, they would not open their eyes. The prophecy of Isaiah was being fulfilled. This quotes the great redemptive chapter of Isaiah 53 which speaks of the death of Christ. Christ's death was presented to them, and they rejected Him. They were blinded to the light which was being presented to them. They were like a man who wakes up in the morning and says to himself, "Today I won't see and I will keep my eyes closed all day." He is just as blind as the man who cannot see. The next quotation is from Isaiah, chapter 6. You may point out that it says, "He hath blinded their eyes, and hardened their heart." That is very true, but this must be taken in its context. Jesus has presented Himself to them as the Messiah and as their King. They have rejected Jesus personally. Now He rejects them! Listen to me carefully. Because they *would* not accept Him, there came the day when they *could* not accept Him. My friend, the most dangerous thing in the world is to hear the gospel and then turn your back on it. If you just go on listening and listening and do not accept it and act upon it, there comes the time when you cannot hear and you cannot see. God is God, and it is He who has the final word.

Nevertheless among the chief rulers also many believed on him; but because of the Pharisees they did not confess him, lest they should be put out of the synagogue:

> For they loved the praise of men more than the praise of
> God [John 12:42–43].

That is unfortunate. They were like secret believers today who are cowards. However, we will find two of these secret believers taking down the body of Jesus from the cross.

> Jesus cried and said, He that believeth on me, believeth
> not on me, but on him that sent me.

> And he that seeth me seeth him that sent me.

> I am come a light into the world, that whosoever be-
> lieveth on me should not abide in darkness [John
> 12:44–46].

Jesus repeats His amazing statement that He is the Light of the World. This is an extension of the time that He opened the eyes of the blind man. He will open the eyes of any who are willing to admit that they are blind and that they need the Light of the World.

> And if any man hear my words, and believe not, I judge
> him not: for I came not to judge the world, but to save the
> world.

> He that rejecteth me, and receiveth not my words, hath
> one that judgeth him: the word that I have spoken, the
> same shall judge him in the last day.

> For I have not spoken of myself; but the Father which
> sent me, he gave me a commandment, what I should say,
> and what I should speak.

> And I know that his commandment is life everlasting:
> whatsoever I speak therefore, even as the Father said
> unto me, so I speak [John 12:47–50].

Friend, we are going to be judged by the Word of God. We will not be judged by our little good works. We will not be judged by what we think religion is. No, we will be judged by the Word of God. Jesus came the first time as the Savior: "I came not to judge the world, but to save the world." The next time He will come as the Judge. The voice from heaven is still saying to us, ". . . This is my beloved Son . . . hear ye him" (Matt. 17:5).

This concludes this section of the Gospel of John. Men had turned their backs on that voice; they had rejected the King. When they had done this, the King rejected them. He is always the King!

CHAPTER 13

THEME: Jesus washes feet of disciples

We come now to the fourth main division of this Gospel. We first studied the prologue, which was the first eighteen verses of chapter 1. Then we had the introduction, which was the remainder of the first chapter. We have seen the Witness of His Works and of His Words from chapters 2 to 12. Now we come to the Witness of Jesus to His Witnesses, chapters 13 to 17.

There is another way in which we could divide this Gospel. In the first twelve chapters the subject is *light*. They tell of His public ministry and that He is the Light. The division which we call the Upper Room Discourse is about the subject of *love*. He loves His own. The last part of the Gospel, from chapters 18 to 21, is about *life*. He came to bring us life, and that life is in Himself. Our life comes through His death.

The Lord Jesus gave four major discourses. Three of these have already been studied in the Gospel of Matthew: the Sermon on the Mount (Matt. 5—7); the Mystery Parables Discourse (Matt. 13), telling us about the Kingdom of Heaven; and the Olivet Discourse (Matt. 24; 25). Now we come to the Upper Room Discourse which is recorded in John 13—17.

This discourse is one of the greatest that our Lord ever gave. It is the longest, and it is meaningful for us today because He took His own into the Upper Room and revealed new truths to them. It is still brand new and fresh for us today. There is nothing quite like it. His public ministry has ended, and He has been rejected. Now He talks about His love for us, how we are to live the Christian life, of the provision He has made for us, and of the relationships between Him and those who are His own. As He is on His way to the Cross, He has no message for the Pharisees or the religious rulers or the Roman government. This message is for His own.

JESUS WASHES FEET OF DISCIPLES

We come now to a most unusual incident. I wish I could shock you, startle you with it. We hear it so often that we lose the wonder of it. Jesus Christ leaves heaven's glory and comes down to this earth and He takes the place of a slave and washes feet!

In the preceding chapter, you will remember, we saw that the feet of Jesus were anointed. Here, the feet of the disciples are washed. What a difference! As the Savior passed through this sinful world, He contacted no defilement whatsoever. He was holy, harmless, and undefiled. The feet speak of the walk of a person, and the anointing of Jesus' feet with spikenard tells of the sweet savor of the walk of our Lord.

The disciples' feet needed washing! Jesus washed their feet with water, not with blood. That is important to see. I hear many people talking about coming anew to the fountain filled with blood and being cleansed. This dishonors our Lord. The blood of Jesus Christ, God's Son, cleanses us from all sin—past, present, and future—in one application. There is only one sacrifice. "For by one offering he hath perfected for ever them that are sanctified" (Heb. 10:14). When you and I came as sinners to Christ Jesus, it was His shed blood that once and for all cleansed us and gave us a standing before God. But, my friend, we need to be purified along the pilgrim pathway; in our walk through the world we get dirty, and we need washing. We shall see that our Lord washed His disciples' feet for this very definite purpose.

There is a threefold reason given to explain why He washed their feet, and we shall note this as we read.

Now before the feast of the passover, when Jesus knew that his hour was come that he should depart out of this world unto the Father, having loved his own which were in the world, he loved them unto the end.

And supper being ended, the devil having now put into the heart of Judas Iscariot, Simon's son, to betray him [John 13:1–2].

Jesus washed their feet because He knew that He would "depart out of this world." His ministry would continue after He went back to heaven. He has identified Himself with His people, and today He still washes the feet of His disciples. He says that He will depart out of this "world" (*kosmos*), meaning the world system. It is man's world, a world of sin. It is a civilization that is anti-God and anti-Christ, and it is under judgment. Because He is leaving this world, He washes their feet.

The second reason He does this is that He loved His own. He loved them "unto the end." He is going to the Father because He loved His own. He died to save His own, and He lives to keep them saved. We have a wonderful Savior, and He loves us right on through to the very end. God loves us with an everlasting love; we cannot keep Him from loving us.

The third reason is that another person had entered into the room. There was an uninvited guest present. His name was Satan. We speak of thirteen persons in the Upper Room, but actually, there were fourteen because Satan was there. Satan put into the heart of Judas Iscariot to betray Him. Wherever the Devil gets into Christian work, others are affected and the Lord must wash them. He must wash us if we are to have fellowship with Him.

Notice that this took place at the Feast of the Passover. "Supper being ended" is literally "supper being in progress." This is not the Lord's Supper. Actually John does not even record the Lord's Supper. Why does John omit something so important? I think it is because at the time John wrote, there were already Christians who were making a ritual out of the Lord's Supper. There is a great danger in putting importance on a ritual rather than on the person Jesus Christ. It is more important to know the Word of God than it is to partake of Communion. There is no blessing in Communion apart from a knowledge of the Word of God. An apologetics professor, whom I had, said that it was Christ in your heart and bread in your tummy. The bread in your tummy won't be there long; Christ in your heart is the essential. I believe that is why John omits telling about the Lord's Supper.

Jesus knowing that the Father had given all things into

his hands, and that he was come from God, and went to God [John 13:3].

A better translation would be, "Since Jesus knew that the Father had given all things into His hands, that He was come from God, and that He is going to God." It is restated that what He is doing is because He is returning to the Father. That is important.

He riseth from supper, and laid aside his garments; and took a towel, and girded himself.

After that he poureth water into a basin, and began to wash the disciples' feet, and to wipe them with the towel wherewith he was girded [John 13:4–5].

He lays aside His outer garment; that is, He takes off the robe that He is wearing. Then He takes a linen cloth, and He girds Himself with it. This is such a strange thing which He does. He takes the place of a servant. He is girded with the towel of service, and He is ready to wash their feet.

In studying Exodus 21, we learn of a law regarding slaves. A Hebrew slave served his master six years, and he could go free on the seventh year. If, during that time, he had taken a wife and had had children, the master would free him but not his family. However, the slave could choose to stay. If he loved his master and his family, he could stay with them. Then the master would back him up to a door post and bore his ear with an awl which would identify him as a voluntary slave forever. Although he could have gone out free, he stayed because of love. Our Lord Jesus came down to this earth, took upon Himself our humanity, and was made in the likeness of a servant. He did all this because He loved us. He could have gone out free, but He died on the Cross to provide salvation for us. He did this to establish a wonderful relationship for us and to make it possible for us to have fellowship with Him. He has become a slave because He loves us.

Then cometh he to Simon Peter: and Peter saith unto him, Lord, dost thou wash my feet?

Jesus answered and said unto him, What I do thou knowest not now; but thou shalt know hereafter [John 13:6–7].

Some people say that this is a sacrament and that we should practice foot washing. I see nothing wrong with practicing this if the spiritual meaning is not lost. Others say that this is a lesson in humility and is an example to us. There is nothing wrong with that interpretation, but I do not think it goes deep enough. Peter certainly could see this was an example of humility; yet the Lord said, "What I do thou knowest not now; but thou shalt know hereafter."

Peter saith unto him, Thou shalt never wash my feet. Jesus answered him, If I wash thee not, thou hast no part with me [John 13:8].

What did our Lord mean by that? He meant that without this washing there can be no fellowship with Him. This is the Passover Feast which speaks of His death. He arose from the Passover Feast which speaks of His rising in resurrection and going back to heaven. He is girded with the towel of service and He is saying to us, "If I don't wash you, you'll have no part with me." You cannot have fellowship with him, service with Him, without the washing.

How does Christ wash us today? "Wherewithal shall a young man cleanse his way? by taking heed thereto according to thy word" (Ps. 119:9). "Now ye are clean through the word which I have spoken unto you" (John 15:3). ". . . even as Christ also loved the church, and gave himself for it; that he might sanctify and cleanse it with the washing of water by the word" (Eph. 5:25–26). It is the Word of God that will keep the believer clean. And when we sin, how are we cleansed? "If we confess our sins, he is faithful and just to forgive us our sins, and to cleanse us from all unrighteousness" (1 John 1:9). Too many people treat sin as a light matter. My friend, may I say to you, the feet speak of the walk, and when you and I become disobedient, we are not walking in His way. That is sin, and that needs to be confessed.

Simon Peter saith unto him, Lord, not my feet only, but also my hands and my head [John 13:9].

He at first pulls his feet up; then when our Lord says he won't have fellowship with Him, he sticks out his feet—big old fisherman's feet—and he holds out his hands—and they have been strong, calloused hands—and he even held down his head, and said, "not just my feet, but also wash my hands, wash my head." If it means fellowship, Peter wants all he can get of that.

Jesus saith to him, He that is washed needeth not save to wash his feet, but is clean every whit: and ye are clean, but not all [John 13:10].

Now He says, "He that's washed needeth not to be washed." That doesn't make good sense, does it? The reason it doesn't is that He used two different words and, unfortunately, the translators didn't make the distinction (nor do our more recent translations make the distinction), but they are absolutely two different words. He says, ". . . He that is louō." Louō means "bathed." Nipto is the word translated "wash." "He that is bathed needeth not except to wash his feet."

In those days they went to the public bath for their bathing. Then a man would put on his sandals to come home. In his home was a basin of water for him to wash his feet because they had gotten dirty walking through the streets of the city. Not only was there dirt, but in those days the garbage was thrown into the streets. So even though he had just come from a bath, he had to wash his feet when he entered the house.

Our Lord is teaching that when we came to the Cross, when we came to Jesus, we were washed all over. That is the bath, louō, regeneration. When we walk through this world, we are defiled and get dirty. We become disobedient, and sin gets into our lives. I do not believe that any believer goes through a day without getting just a little dirty. He says that we cannot have fellowship with Him if we are dirty. So the washing of the feet, niptō, is the cleansing in order to restore us to fellowship. "If we say that we have fellowship with him, and walk in darkness, we lie, and do not the truth: But if we walk in the light, as he is in the light, we have fellowship one with another, and the blood of Jesus Christ his Son cleanseth us [keeps on cleaning us] from all sin" (1 John 1:6–7).

Friend, in order to have our feet washed we must first confess our sin. To confess means to agree with God. It means to say the same thing that God says about our sin. One of the hardest things in the world is to get a saint to admit he is a sinner. Coldness, indifference, lack of love, all are seen by God as sin. If we confess, He is faithful and just to forgive. But that is not all. If you are going to have your feet washed, you must put them into the hands of the Savior. That is obedience. We can't just say, "God forgive me, I did wrong," and then go out and do the same thing all over again. That's not getting your feet into the hands of the Savior.

> **For he knew who should betray him; therefore said he, Ye are not all clean [John 13:11].**

Jesus knew that Judas would betray Him. He knew that Judas had not taken a bath. In other words, Judas had never been regenerated. That is why He said they were not all clean.

> **So after he had washed their feet, and had taken his garments, and was set down again, he said unto them, Know ye what I have done to you?**

> **Ye call me Master and Lord: and ye say well; for so I am.**

> **If I then, your Lord and Master, have washed your feet; ye also ought to wash one another's feet.**

> **For I have given you an example, that ye should do as I have done to you.**

> **Verily, verily, I say unto you, The servant is not greater than his lord; neither he that is sent greater than he that sent him.**

If ye know these things, happy are ye if ye do them [John 13:12-17].

If you want joy in your life today, Christian friend, go to Him and confess. This is one of the problems in our Christian congregations today. We may have our heads full of doctrine, but our feet smell. Brother, there is nothing that smells as bad as unwashed feet! Maybe that is the reason some of our services don't smell so good. That is the reason we don't reach more people for Christ. We need to confess in order to have fellowship with Christ.

Jesus said that as He had washed their feet, so they were to wash one another's feet. What does that mean? Paul tells us in Galatians how we are to do that. "Brethren, if a man be overtaken in a fault, ye which are spiritual, restore such an one in the spirit of meekness; considering thyself, lest thou also be tempted" (Gal. 6:1). That is, when a brother in Christ falls into sin, he is to be brought back into fellowship by one who is spiritual. Beating him on the head and criticizing him is not washing his feet, friend. To restore him means to wash his feet. In the church we have all sorts of talent—excellent speakers and beautiful music—but there is no revival. We need foot washing; we need to be cleansed. Before we can wash the feet of a brother, we need first to have the Lord of glory wash our feet. We should come to Him every time that we are dirty and be cleansed by Him.

The psalmist says, "Search me, O God, and know my heart: try me, and know my thoughts: and see if there be any wicked way in me, and lead me in the way everlasting" (Ps. 139:23-24). There is not a one of us who goes through a day without some sin. We need to confess that to the Lord and be cleansed. We are washed by the Word of God. We put our feet into His hands, which means that we are completely yielded to Him. This places us in fellowship with the Lord Jesus. Friend, don't let a single day go by without this fellowship. Don't let sin come in to break this fellowship with Him.

The disciples were like a group of children in that Upper Room. They were frightened, and rightly so. The shadow of the Cross had fallen upon that little group.

I speak not of you all: I know whom I have chosen: but that the scripture may be fulfilled, He that eateth bread with me hath lifted up his heel against me [John 13:18].

Jesus is very careful to tell them that He does not speak of all of them. He has just told them they are happy if they do these things, but there is one man among them who cannot do them. Do you know why? He has not believed. Jesus has already told them that all of them are not clean. Jesus had said, "Ye call me Master and Lord." A master is a teacher and he is to be believed. A lord is to be obeyed. Faith and obedience must go together. Saving, living faith leads to obedience. Judas did not have this faith.

Jesus quotes Psalm 41:9: ". . . which did eat of my bread, hath lifted up his heel against me." He is referring to Judas. It is not a question of this man losing his spiritual life. It is rather a revelation that he never had a spiritual life! He is not a sheep who has become unclean; he is a pig that has returned to its wallowing again, or a dog that has returned to its vomit. That is the picture of Judas Iscariot. Yet, he was there in the Upper Room and this man got his feet washed. He received the washing by the Word of God, and he rejected it totally.

Let us go over this again so it is very clear. The blood of Jesus Christ is the Godward side of His sacrifice. The blood is for the expiation of our sin. The blood has cancelled all my guilt and has washed out that awful, black account which was against me. It has given me a standing before God because it has blotted out all my transgressions. The blood is for penal expiation. The cleansing by the water is the manward aspect of it. This is for our moral purification. After we have our standing before God on the ground of the blood of Jesus Christ, the water of the Word gives us our moral purification in our daily walk.

Now I tell you before it come, that, when it is come to pass, ye may believe that I am he [John 13:19].

Jesus tells them that one of them will "lift up his heel" against Him so that when it happens, they will not be shocked. Then they cannot say it was a pity Jesus didn't know about it. Have you ever noticed that the

Lord Jesus is betrayed from the inside? This is still true today. People complain about the sin outside the church, but that doesn't hurt the church. In fact, some of those sinners get saved. The hurt comes when Jesus Christ is betrayed on the inside.

> **Verily, verily, I say unto you, He that receiveth whomsoever I send receiveth me; and he that receiveth me receiveth him that sent me [John 13:20].**

Jesus adds this because Judas had been sent on missions with the rest of the disciples. He had preached and he had healed. "He that receiveth whomsoever I send receiveth me; and he that receiveth me receiveth him that sent me." No one is saved by the faith of the messenger or preacher. We are saved by hearing the Word of God and receiving Christ. If a Western Union boy brings you a telegram that a rich uncle has died and left you a fortune, the fact that the Western Union boy may be a thief doesn't invalidate the message of the telegram, does it?

I knew a preacher who had become an unbeliever. A man who drove me to the train said to me, "Dr. McGee, I am puzzled. I was saved under the ministry of that man. I know I am saved and I know I am a child of God but I am puzzled. How can you explain it?" I showed this man this very text and told him that even Judas had gone out preaching and had won converts, not because he was Judas, but because he had given the message. God will bless His Word. We are saved by hearing the Word.

> **When Jesus had thus said, he was troubled in spirit, and testified, and said, Verily, verily, I say unto you, that one of you shall betray me.**
>
> **Then the disciples looked one on another, doubting of whom he spake.**
>
> **Now there was leaning on Jesus' bosom one of his disciples, whom Jesus loved.**

Simon Peter therefore beckoned to him, that he should ask who it should be of whom he spake.

He then lying on Jesus' breast saith unto him, Lord, who is it? [John 13:21–25].

If you think that Jesus was unmoved because Judas was going to betray Him, you are wrong. He was *troubled* in spirit. The disciples were stupefied. You can imagine the shock wave that went over that room. Judas had been so clever that not a person there believed he was the traitor. Each one thought it might be the other, and each one thought it might be himself. Each disciple knew that he was capable of doing the same thing.

I doubt that the little by-play between John and Peter was noticed by the others. There must have been confusion in the room. Peter was probably farther away from Jesus, and since John was next to Him, Peter signaled to John to ask.

Jesus answered, He it is, to whom I shall give a sop, when I have dipped it. And when he had dipped the sop, he gave it to Judas Iscariot, the Son of Simon [John 13:26].

It was the custom for the host at a banquet to take a piece of bread, dip it in the sauce, and present it to the guest of honor. The Lord makes Judas His guest of honor by this gesture. He is extending to him the token of friendship. Judas is at the crossroads. Christ keeps the door open to Judas up to the very last. Even in the garden Jesus will say, ". . . Friend, wherefore art thou come? . . ." (Matt. 26:50)—still keeping the door open for Judas.

Jesus knew what Judas would do. As another has stated it, "foreknowledge is not causation." That is, although the Lord knew what Judas would do, the Lord did not force him to do it. In fact, He offered His friendship to Judas to the very last.

**And after the sop Satan entered into him. Then said
Jesus unto him, That thou doest, do quickly [John
13:27].**

Satan took over this man Judas gradually. I don't think that Satan ever
takes a man suddenly. There are many little falls that permit Satan to
move in gradually. Then finally he takes over. The Lord gave Judas an
opportunity to accept Him, but Judas turned his back on the Lord.
Then Satan moved in and took him over completely.

Judas makes his own decision. God never sends a man to hell unless that man first of all sends himself there. You see, God ratifies
human decision; God seconds the motion. When a man says that he
accepts Christ, God says, "I second it; I receive you." When a man
says that he rejects Christ, as Judas did here, God says, "I second the
motion."

Now Jesus asks him to leave quickly. Having made his decision, he
is not beyond the control of God. In fact, having made his decision, he
is compelled to cooperate with God. You see, the religious rulers
didn't want to arrest Jesus and crucify Him while the crowds were
there during the feast. They wanted to wait until the feast was over.
But our Lord tells him to go now and do it quickly. So Judas must go
out and tell the leaders that he has been found out, and they must
move quickly.

**Now no man at the table knew for what intent he spake
this unto him [John 13:28].**

No one at the table even suspected that Judas was the betrayer.

**For some of them thought, because Judas had the bag,
that Jesus had said unto him, Buy those things that we
have need of against the feast; or, that he should give
something to the poor [John 13:29].**

Notice that our Lord did not beg for support. They had a treasury, and
they carried on their business in a businesslike way. It also tells us that

the Lord did not feed them miraculously. They had to go and buy food. They were not some "far out" group. Judas was the treasurer. There is always a temptation in the handling of money—which is equally true today. At the Passover season donations were given to the poor; so the disciples thought this may have been what the Lord asked him to do with the money.

> **He then having received the sop went immediately out: and it was night [John 13:30].**

Notice also that when Judas went out, it was night. Friend, it was eternal night for Judas. It was the Devil's day, and the Devil's day is always like the darkness that descended on Egypt. This man walked out into eternal night.

What God does, He does slowly. What the Devil does, he does quickly. The Devil must move fast because his days are limited. God has all eternity to accomplish His purposes. Often we fail to understand that.

There is now a change in the room. Judas is gone, and our Lord begins to talk to these men. They are frightened. The shadow of the Cross is over that little group in the Upper Room. Now our Lord attempts to lift these men from the low plane to the high plane; from the here-and-now to the hereafter; from the material to the eternal; from that which is secular to that which is spiritual. Although Simon Peter interrupts Him, I think Jesus' discourse begins right here and goes on into chapter 14.

> **Therefore, when he was gone out, Jesus said, Now is the Son of man glorified, and God is glorified in him.**
>
> **If God be glorified in him, God shall also glorify him in himself, and shall straightway glorify him [John 13:31–32].**

The Lord Jesus is now moving into the spiritual realm. The Son of Man is going to be glorified, and this will be accomplished through

His death and resurrection. From the human side the Cross looks like shame and defeat, but God is glorified in Him because the salvation of the world will be wrought through the Cross.

> **Little children, yet a little while I am with you. Ye shall seek me: and as I said unto the Jews, Whither I go, ye cannot come; so now I say to you [John 13:33].**

Judas is gone now so He can address them as His little children. He is going to the Cross, and no one can go to the Cross as He did. He suffered alone, and there is a suffering of Christ which you and I cannot fully comprehend.

> **A new commandment I give unto you, That ye love one another; as I have loved you, that ye also love one another.**
>
> **By this shall all men know that ye are my disciples, if ye have love one to another [John 13:34–35].**

Now He gives to them a new commandment. Some folk would seem to think that He said, "By this shall all men know that ye are my disciples, if you are *fundamental* in the faith." Now friend, I believe in being fundamental in the faith, I believe in the inerrancy of the Word of God, in the verbal, plenary inspiration of the Scriptures, in the deity of the Lord Jesus Christ. I believe that He died on the Cross for the expiation of sin; that He died a substitutionary, vicarious death for the sins of the world. I believe He was raised bodily and ascended back into heaven and that He is coming personally to take His church out of the world. But I want to say this, and I want to say it very carefully: believing those things does not convince the unsaved world outside. The world is dying for just a little love. Jesus says that His disciples are to be known for their love.

When I was a boy, my dad died and I went to work to support my mother and sister; so I stayed with two aunts and a bachelor uncle. One aunt was a Baptist and the other a Presbyterian. My uncle was an unbeliever and a beer drinker. Every Sunday he would get up just in time for the noon meal. For dinner every Sunday we heard all the Baptist dirt and the Presbyterian dirt. Years later, when my uncle was in the hospital, one of my aunts wept and asked me, "Vernon, why doesn't he come to Christ?" I almost told her. Friend, may I say, we do not win the lost by being Christian cannibals. "But if ye bite and devour one another, take heed that ye be not consumed one of another" (Gal. 5:15). This is the type of thing that is turning the unsaved away from the church today. This is the reason they don't come in to hear the gospel. They hear the gossip before they can hear the gospel! Do you realize that the most important commandment for a Christian is not to witness, not to serve, but to *love* other believers?

Tertullian writes that the Roman government was disturbed about the early church. Christians were increasing in number by leaps and bounds. Because they wouldn't take even a pinch of incense and put it before the image of the emperor, the Romans felt they might be disloyal. Spies went into the Christian gathering and came back with a report something like this: "These Christians are very strange people. They meet together in an empty room to worship. They do not have an image. They speak of One by the name of Jesus, who is absent, but whom they seem to be expecting at any time. And my, how they love Him and how they love one another." Now if spies came from an atheistic government to see whether Christianity is genuine and they came to your church, what would be the verdict? Would they go back to report how these Christians love each other?

Simon Peter said unto him, Lord, whither goest thou? Jesus answered him, Whither I go, thou canst not follow me now; but thou shalt follow me afterwards.

Peter said unto him, Lord, why cannot I follow thee now? I will lay down my life for thy sake.

Jesus answered him, Wilt thou lay down thy life for my sake? Verily, verily, I say unto thee, The cock shall not crow, till thou hast denied me thrice [John 13:36-38].

Here is a man who is close to all of us. I believe that if you are a child of God, you would never sell out Jesus as Judas did. The Devil does not have control of you, because the Spirit of God dwells in you. But there isn't a one of us who would not do what Simon Peter did. His problem was not that Satan was in his heart but that he had confidence in his own flesh. I believe that is the problem for all of us.

Peter really loved the Lord. Peter was ready to defend the Lord. Yet the Lord must treat Peter as a juvenile. He is always blundering—I don't believe this man reached mental and spiritual maturity until the Day of Pentecost. The only things he heard of all that Jesus had said was that Jesus was going away. He reacts like a child who says, "Where are you going, Daddy? I want to go, too." His first question is, "Lord, whither goest thou?" His second is, "Lord, why cannot I follow thee now?"

When Jesus answered him, "Whither I go, thou canst not follow me now; but thou shalt follow me afterwards," the only thing that Peter heard was the "now." He is like a child who asks for a cookie. When the mother says he cannot have the cookie now but must wait until after dinner, the child seizes on the "now." He wants the cookie now. He doesn't want to wait until after dinner.

Peter's love for and loyalty to Jesus was sincere. He wanted to follow the Lord wherever He was going. When he said, "I will lay down my life for thy sake," he meant every word of it. He attempted to fight for his Lord, and he cut off the servant's ear. (The reason he got his ear was because he was a fisherman and not a swordsman. He was aiming for his head.) When the Lord told Peter that he would deny Him three times before the cock would crow, it was already dark, and he just couldn't believe he would deny his Lord before the dawn.

What a lesson there is here for us. Peter was overconfident in himself. We should learn from this that we should have no confidence in the flesh. Paul says, ". . . when I am weak, then am I strong" (2 Cor.

12:10). Do you recognize your weakness or do you think you are strong? Someone asked Dwight L. Moody, "Do you have grace enough to die for Jesus?" He answered, "No, He hasn't asked me to do that. But if He asks me to, I know He will give me the grace to do it." That is the answer. Our own flesh is weak, but God will supply our every need.

CHAPTER 14

THEME: Jesus comforts His disciples

Chapter divisions in the Bible are wonderful because they help us find our way around in the Bible, but sometimes the chapter break is at an unfortunate place, as is the case here. What our Lord says at the beginning of chapter 14 is a continuation of what He was saying to Simon Peter in chapter 13.

Simon Peter has just declared that he would lay down his life for Him. Then the Lord Jesus told him that he would deny Him three times by the time the rooster crowed in the morning. We will see later that, when the rooster crowed that morning, Simon Peter had denied Him three times. Still speaking to Simon Peter, our Lord gave this chapter to bring him through that dark night of denial and to bring him back into a right relationship with God. It was given to comfort him. This chapter has cushioned the shock for multitudes of people from that day right down to the present hour.

JESUS COMFORTS HIS DISCIPLES

Let not your heart be troubled: ye believe in God, believe also in me [John 14:1].

People all over the world are seeking comfort at this very moment. They long for peace in their hearts. Jesus alone can bring that comfort, and here He tells the basis for it: "ye believe in God, believe also in me." In the Greek, this can also be an imperative or a command. Believe in God. Believe in Me also.

With the word *believe* we find the preposition *eis* which means "into." When John talks about saving faith, there is always a preposition with it. The faith is not inactive, not passive; it is to believe *into* or to believe *upon* or to believe *in*. It is an active faith, which is trust. If you believe that your car will take you home, how do you get home?

By just believing it? No, you believe in it so much that you commit yourself to the car. You get into it and trust that it will get you home. In just such a way you get saved. You believe in Christ; you trust yourself to Him.

"Ye believe in God, believe also in me" is a clear-cut statement of our Lord that He is God. I know a theology professor who claims that Jesus did not claim deity. I'd like to know what He is saying here in this first verse if He is not making Himself equal with God. His statement makes something very clear right here. To believe in God means you are not an atheist, but to be a *Christian*, you must have personal faith and trust in Christ.

> **In my Father's house are many mansions: if it were not
> so, I would have told you. I go to prepare a place for you
> [John 14:2].**

Let's establish, first of all, what the Father's house is; the Father's house is this vast universe that you and I live in today. We are living on one of the very minor, smallest planets. We're just a speck in space. We live in the Father's house.

Sir James Jeans called it the expanding universe. First, men thought of the earth with the stars up there like electric light bulbs screwed in the top of the universe. Then men began to explore and found that we are in a solar system, that we are actually a minor planet going around the sun, and that there are quite a few other planets "tripping the light fantastic" around the sun with us. We, together with other solar systems, are in a galactic system, and when you look up at the Milky Way, you see the other side of our galactic system. Now friend, ours is only one galactic system. If we could move out far enough, we would find other galactic systems that make ours look like it is just a peanut in space. We are told that our nearest neighbor, Andromeda, is something like 2,000,000 light years away from us. Friend, we won't go to our nearest neighbor of the galactic system to borrow a cup of sugar in the morning, because we won't get back in time for lunch! Even these galactic systems are not the end of space at all. Beyond them, they find what they call quasars. The reason the astronomers call them quasars is because that is a German word meaning they don't know what they are. They have found them through the radio telescopes like they have on the Mojave Desert. They have an even bigger telescope over in England, and they have found that beyond these quasars are other—well, they don't know what they are—so the British have come up with the very fine scientific term, "blops," and so they call them blops! We simply do not know how vast this universe is. It may be an infinite universe. If there is an infinite universe, there must be an infinite God. Maybe God is letting us paint ourselves into a corner so that we will have to acknowledge that He is up there after all!

Our Lord said, "In my Father's house are many mansions." I think there was a wry smile on His face when He said that. He is the One who made them, and He knew how many there were out there. We don't know and may never know. I do not think that God has a vacancy sign hanging out anyplace in this vast universe. I don't mean that human beings are living on other planets. One is enough of little mankind—we are the ones who are in rebellion against God. However, I think this vast universe is filled with created intelligences who are looking at this little earth. This is where they see something unique in the universe. They knew something about God's wisdom and His person and His power, but they knew nothing about His love until the second Person of the Trinity came down to this earth and died on the Cross. God so loved the world that He gave His only begotten Son! There is a display of God's love on this earth.

You and I think we are pretty valuable. I don't want to offend anybody, friend, but do you know the human race isn't worth saving? God could very easily brush us off this little earth and start over again. He could speak the earth and us out of existence and very little would be missing. But then He wouldn't be demonstrating His love. He would be demonstrating justice and righteousness but not love. God loves us. That is the amazing thing and the most wonderful thing in the world. God loves us! He loves you and me, not because we are worth loving, but He loves us in spite of the fact that we are absolutely, totally depraved. We belong to that kind of human race. If you deny that, look around you. Unless there is something radically wrong with the human family, how could a civilization that reached such heights tumble as far as we have gone in two or three decades?

"In my Father's house are many mansions." For many years I was an ordained Presbyterian preacher, and I lived in what that church calls a "manse," which is a shortened form of *mansion.* I lived in my first manse before I was married. It was a big place with fourteen rooms, and on a clear day you could see the ceiling in the living room. It was cold, and I lived in one corner of a room near the fire. When anybody talks to me about a mansion in the sky, I shudder. The Greek word is *monē* meaning "abiding places." Jesus is saying that this vast universe is filled with abiding places or places to live.

"If it were not so, I would have told you." The Lord Jesus puts His entire reputation on the line here, and you either believe Him or you don't believe Him, my friend. "I go to prepare a place for you." This is quite wonderful. This vast universe is filled with so many places; yet He has gone to prepare a place for those who are His own. I said I think the universe is filled with intelligent creatures. John got a look at some of them in the Book of Revelation, and he was overwhelmed. He said there are a thousand times ten thousand; then he saw more and added thousands of thousands. We are dealing with a tremendous and wonderful God. One can look upon the millions in this world today and wonder whether we will get lost in the shuffle somewhere. But Jesus is up there preparing a place for all of us who belong to Him. No one can occupy it but us.

Years ago a neighbor of mine was one of the men working on the mirror for the 200-inch telescope at Palomar. In grinding the mirror, they missed it the first time by, I think, a millionth of an inch. When they finally got it finished, I kept asking him what they were seeing. Finally, he got tired of my constant questioning and wanted to know why I was so interested. "Well," I said, "you've got that big eye poked in the front window of my Father's house, and I'd like to know what you're seeing, because Jesus is preparing a place for me up there."

And if I go and prepare a place for you, I will come again, and receive you unto myself; that where I am, there ye may be also [John 14:3].

This is the first time in the Bible where you find a mention of God taking anyone off this earth to go out yonder to a place that He has prepared. This was not the hope of the Old Testament saint. God never promised Abraham to take him off yonder to a star. God told him He would make his offspring as numerous as the stars, but the promise to Abraham was to give him an eternal home on this earth. The hope of the Old Testament was for a kingdom down here on this earth in which would dwell peace and righteousness. This is the fulfillment of God's purpose for this earth. Personally, I think the expression "the Kingdom of Heaven" means the reign of God over this earth. God has said, "Yet have I set my king upon my holy hill of Zion" (Ps. 2:6). That is God's earthly purpose, and He is moving undeviatingly, unhesitatingly, and uncompromisingly toward the day when He puts His own Son upon the throne here on earth. That will be the Kingdom of Heaven. That is God's earthly purpose; it is the hope of the Old Testament.

The disciples are startled when Jesus reveals that He is going to take a people—beginning with the apostles—off this earth to be with Christ in the place that He is preparing for them. This is the first time it is mentioned, but it is not the last time. Paul talked about it, saying in 1 Thessalonians 4 that the Lord Himself would descend from heaven with a shout. His voice will be like a trumpet and like the sound of an archangel. He is coming to call His own. The dead in Christ will rise first, and then those believers who are still alive will be caught up together to meet the Lord in the air. So shall we ever be with the Lord in that place that He has prepared. John, in Revelation 21, tells us that the city, the new Jerusalem, will come down from God out of heaven. It will be a new city, a new concept in urban dwelling, my friend, and that is where believers, from the apostles on, will dwell throughout eternity.

And whither I go ye know, and the way ye know [John 14:4].

He is lifting these men into the heights, because, you see, there in the Upper Room the shadow of the Cross had fallen athwart that company, and sin was knocking at the door of that room demanding its pound of flesh. Our Lord is attempting to lift them from the here-and-now to the hereafter, from the material to the spiritual, from the earthly to the heavenly. Jesus tells them two things: the destination, which is the "where," and the way to go, which is the "how."

Thomas saith unto him, Lord, we know not whither thou goest; and how can we know the way? [John 14:5].

There is an apostle sitting there whom we call doubting Thomas. He seems always to be asking a question or raising a doubt. He had a question mark for a brain, and it took our Lord a long time to make an exclamation mark out of it! I am really glad that he was there and that he asked the question, because it is a good question. I would have wanted to ask it if I had been there. If he hadn't asked the question, we would never have had our Lord's wonderful answer, which is the gospel in a nutshell.

Jesus saith unto him, I am the way, the truth, and the life: no man cometh unto the Father, but by me [John 14:6].

The article in the Greek is an adjective. Jesus said, "I am the way." He is not just a person who shows the way, but He, personally, is the way. No church or ceremony can bring you to God. Only Christ can bring you to God. He is the way. Either you have Christ or you don't have Him; either you trust Him or you don't. Also Jesus said that He is the truth. He isn't saying that He tells the truth, although He does do that. He is the truth! He is the bureau of standards for truth, the very touchstone of truth. And He is the life. He isn't simply stating that He is alive. He is the source, the origin of life from the lowest vegetable plane of life to the highest spiritual plane of life.

"No man cometh unto the Father, but by me." He made a dead-end street of all the cults and "isms." He says the only way to God is through Him. That is a dogmatic statement! Years ago a student out at UCLA told me he didn't like the Bible because it is filled with dogmatism. I agreed with him that it is. He especially selected this verse and said, "That's dogmatic." I said, "It sure is, but have you realized that it is characteristic of truth to be dogmatic? Truth has to be dogmatic."

I had a teacher who was the most dogmatic, narrow-minded person I've ever met. She insisted that 2 plus 2 = 4. It didn't make any difference what you had two of—apples or cows or dollars—she always insisted that $2 + 2 = 4$. She was dogmatic. I have found that the bank I do business with operates on the same principle. Only in my case it is $2 - 2 = 0$, and they are dogmatic about it. Friend, let me say to you that one of the characteristics of truth is its dogmatism.

Now, not all dogmatism is truth—there is a lot of ignorance that is dogmatic. However, that which is truth has to be dogmatic. When I ask directions to go somewhere, I do not want my directions from a man who isn't sure and doesn't know exactly how to get there. I want my directions from one who knows exactly where I'm to turn and how many blocks I'm to go. As I said to this young student, "Millions of people for over nineteen hundred years have been coming to Christ on the basis of His statement, 'I am the way,' and they have found it is accurate, that it has brought them to heaven. Why don't you try it? The Lord Jesus says you are not going to get to heaven except through Him. Why not come through Him and make sure?"

Someday I hope I can thank the apostle Thomas for asking our Lord this question in the Upper Room: "How can we know the way?" Without it we would not have this marvelous answer in John 14:6.

Now there is another interruption. Philip has a question.

If ye had known me, ye should have known my Father also: and from henceforth ye know him, and have seen him.

Philip saith unto him, Lord, shew us the Father, and it sufficeth us [John 14:7–8].

Philip was a very quiet individual, the opposite from loquacious Peter. I think he spoke very seldom. He has a Greek name and some Bible students believe that he was a Greek. However, he could have been Jewish and still have a Greek name. He is a very unusual man because every time we meet him he is bringing someone to Jesus. Remember that he brought Nathanael. I've often wondered about that. Philip was the quiet man and Nathanael was the wisecracker. Philip was the straight man and Nathanael was the humorist. But quiet Philip brings people to Jesus. Remember that the Greeks came to him, wanting to see Jesus. Here he expresses the highest ambition any man can have, the highest desire expressed by any person in the whole Bible, "shew us the Father."

I'd like to ask you a personal question today. What is your desire in life? What is your ultimate goal? Do you want to get rich? Do you want to make a name for yourself? Do you want to educate your children? Do you want to bring them up in the discipline and instruction of the Lord? Our goals may be worthy goals; yet the highest goal is this expressed by Philip, "Lord, shew us the Father."

Jesus saith unto him, Have I been so long time with you, and yet hast thou not known me, Philip? he that hath seen me hath seen the Father; and how sayest thou then, Shew us the Father? [John 14:9].

Philip knew from the Old Testament that Moses had seen the glory of God and that Isaiah had a vision of the glory of God. I don't think that we should interpret Jesus' answer as a rebuke. He tells Philip that He has performed many miracles. Although Philip had not seen the glory of God as Moses or Isaiah did, he had seen Jesus and had witnessed His words and His works. Everything that Philip wished to see, he had seen in Jesus Christ. He had seen God. In Christ there is a much greater revelation of God than anything in the Old Testament. Philip had the greatest revelation of God because he had seen Him incarnate in flesh and been with Him—in His presence—for three years! Remember that the writer to the Hebrews says that Jesus is the brightness of the Father's glory and the express image of His person (see Heb. 1:3). "He that hath seen me hath seen the Father" does not mean you are seeing the identical Person, but you are seeing the same Person in power, in character, in love, and in everything else. You have seen all you would see in God the Father because "God is a Spirit: and they that worship him must worship him in spirit and in truth" (John 4:24). "No man hath seen God at any time; the only begotten Son, which is in the bosom of the Father, he hath declared him" (John 1:18). It is Jesus Christ whom we see. We are going to spend all eternity with Him. For those of us who love Him, the goal of our lives is to come to know Him.

> **Believest thou not that I am in the Father, and the Father in me? the words that I speak unto you I speak not of myself: but the Father that dwelleth in me, he doeth the works [John 14:10].**

Jesus here points to the testimony of His words and of His works. They are the same. One equals the other. He was perfectly consistent. You see, our problem is to get our words and our works synchronized. We make tremendous statements and give glorious testimonies, but none of us lives a perfect life. This is the reason every Christian should have a time of confession. As we saw in chapter 13, Jesus says that He must wash us so that we may have fellowship with Him. Too many Christians lose their fellowship with God because they think they are all right, but their words and their works are not consistent. This needs to be confessed.

Have you ever noticed that the Lord Jesus never appealed to His own mind and His own will to make a decision? "The words that I speak unto you I speak not of myself: but the Father that dwelleth in me, he doeth the works." When He spoke, it was the will of the Father. All His works were the will of the Father. So He tells Philip that when he heard the words of Jesus, he was hearing the words of the Father and, when he saw the works of Jesus, he was seeing the Father working through Jesus.

You will notice that Jesus has interruptions during His discourse. First it was Peter, then Thomas, and now Philip. But Jesus continues on in His discourse until verse 22 when He is again interrupted.

> **Believe me that I am in the Father, and the Father in me: or else believe me for the very works' sake [John 14:11].**

Jesus says that if you can't believe Him because of His words, then believe Him because of His works. They should convince you.

> **Verily, verily, I say unto you, He that believeth on me, the works that I do shall he do also; and greater works than these shall he do; because I go unto my Father [John 14:12].**

To understand this verse, I should call attention to the fact that the second word *works* is in italics which means that it is not in the better manuscripts but is put in by the translators to fill out the thought. To be accurate, it should read: "the works that I do shall he do also; and greater than these shall he do." When our Lord was down here on this earth, He performed tremendous works and miracles. These apostles to whom He spoke did the same things. They healed the sick and raised the dead. Yet Jesus says that those who believe on Him will do greater. What is the greater thing which they shall do?

Simon Peter, who had denied Him on the night He was arrested, preached a sermon on the Day of Pentecost and 3000 people became believers! I think of the men over the years who have invested their lives in winning men to Christ. I think of missionaries, such as George L. Mackey who went to Uganda. What a missionary he was! Preaching a crucified, risen, glorified, returning Savior so that a hearer may accept Christ and be born again is a greater miracle than healing the sick. Am I right? Which is better: to heal the soul or to heal the body? When Jesus Christ was on earth, He performed the miracle of raising the physical bodies of men, but we have the privilege of preaching Jesus Christ so that men, body and soul, may live eternally. The supreme accomplishment is to bring men and women into a right relationship with God.

How are these greater works done? "Because I go unto my Father." You see, it is *Christ* who is still working, but today He is working through human instrumentality. He works through frail human clay, human flesh. I am amazed that I can give a Bible message over the radio and there are people who turn to Christ. Friend, that is greater. If Jesus Christ were here speaking to people, it would be a great work.

When Jesus Christ takes you and me and works through us to reach people, that is greater.

Have you noticed how often Jesus speaks of His Father? The Father is mentioned twenty times in this passage, and it is always the Lord Jesus who mentions Him.

And whatsoever ye shall ask in my name, that will I do, that the Father may be glorified in the Son.

If ye shall ask any thing in my name, I will do it [John 14:13–14].

He continues right on to say that these greater things are the result of prayer. Prayer evangelism is so neglected today. "Whatsoever ye shall ask in my name, that will I do."

These verses have been so misunderstood. A great many people have picked this up like a dog picks up a bone and runs with it. They say they prayed and God just didn't answer their prayer. I've had Christian people tell me that they took that verse at face value. They prayed and God didn't answer their prayer. They ask me what is wrong. I tell them that they are reading something into the verse that is not there at all. They need to keep on reading. This is all tied into one package.

If ye love me, keep my commandments [John 14:15].

Now let us consider what all three of these verses say. What does it mean to ask in the name of Christ? To pray in His Person means to be standing in His place. It means to be fully identified with Him, joined to Christ. It means that you and I are pleading the merits of His blessed Son when we stand before God. We have no standing of our own before God at all. He does not hear my prayer because I am Vernon McGee, and He does not hear your prayer because you are who you are. He hears our prayers when they are in the name of Christ. This is not just a little phrase that we tag on to the end of our prayer closing with "in Jesus' name." Praying in His name is presenting it in His merit and for His glory.

"That will I do, that the Father may be glorified in the Son." A prayer that will enable God to be glorified in the Son is the prayer that He will answer. So, when we pray in the name of Jesus and for the glory of God, we are not praying for something selfishly for ourselves. We are praying for Him. We are praying that the Father may be glorified in the Son.

Also it depends on our obedience to Christ. This promise is given to those who love Him, and the evidence of their love is the keeping of His commandments. Love will be demonstrated by obedience to Christ. An undisciplined Christian cannot say that he loves the Lord Jesus. How are you doing in that area, friend? Do you love Him? Are you keeping His commandments because you love Him today?

Dr. Harry Ironside was sitting on a platform with a young pastor during a meeting one night. A young lady entered the meeting and the pastor told him that she formerly had been an active leader among his members, then had begun to run with the world, and that this was the first time he had seen her in church in months. Dr. Ironside preached on this passage of Scripture that night. She was greatly incensed and came to see him after the meeting. "How dare you tell these people that if you ask anything in the name of Jesus, He will do it?" she asked him. Dr. Ironside answered, "Why don't you sit down and tell me about it?" She told him that her father had been desperately ill some months before, and while the doctor was up in his room, she had knelt in the living room, claimed that promise, and prayed in Jesus' name for his recovery. When the doctor came down from the room, he told her that her father was dead. "Now," she said, "don't tell me that God keeps His promises!" Dr. Ironside said, "Did you read the next verse, 'If ye love me, keep my commandments'?" Then Dr. Ironside asked her what would happen if she found a check made out to someone else and tried to cash it by signing that name. She said "I would be a forger." So he referred her to this verse, "If ye love me, keep my commandments." Then he asked her, "Have you been doing that?" Instead of replying, she turned red. Then he explained that what she was trying to do was the same thing as trying to cash a check made out to somebody else. We all need to recognize, friend, that obedience to

Him is the evidence of our love for Him, and this promise is given to those who love Him.

> **And I will pray the Father, and he shall give you another Comforter, that he may abide with you for ever;**
>
> **Even the Spirit of truth; whom the world cannot receive, because it seeth him not, neither knoweth him: but ye know him; for he dwelleth with you, and shall be in you [John 14:16–17].**

This is a unique fact of this age in which we are living. The Holy Spirit was here on earth before Pentecost, but on the Day of Pentecost He came to indwell believers. That was the thing which was new.

"Holy" and "Spirit" describe Him, but *Comforter* is His name, if He has a name. It is a very fitting name, as *com* means "along side of" and *fortis* means "strong." He is the strong One who abides with us forever.

He does not say that the world *would not* receive the Spirit of truth. He says the world *cannot* receive Him. Oh, if we could learn this! The Spirit of God can take the Word of God and open it to the believer, but the unsaved man must first believe in Jesus Christ as his Savior. The man of the world cannot see Him because He is seen and worshiped in spirit and truth. He is seen with the spiritual eye. It is only by the Spirit of God that these eyes and ears can be opened to understand the Word of God. The Holy Spirit is the teacher to lead and guide us into truth. Without Him, the Bible becomes a book of history, a book of facts. The Holy Spirit teaches the truths of the Bible. The Holy Spirit has been in the world, but Jesus says that now He "shall be in you."

> **I will not leave you comfortless: I will come to you [John 14:18].**

The Greek word for *comfortless* is *orphanos* which means "orphans." Jesus says that He will not leave us orphans but will come to us in the person of the Holy Spirit.

Yet a little while, and the world seeth me no more; but ye see me: because I live, ye shall live also.

At that day ye shall know that I am in my Father, and ye in me, and I in you [John 14:19-20].

What is "that day?" It is the day you and I are living in. It is the day that began with Pentecost.

"Ye in me, and I in you" is the most profound statement in the Gospel of John or in the whole Bible. They are all monosyllabic words so that a little child can understand them; yet no philosopher can plumb the depths of their meaning. "You in Me"—that is salvation. To be saved means to be in Christ. That is why Peter says that we are saved by baptism. Baptism means identification, and it means to be identified with Christ. God sees everyone as either in Christ or out of Christ. You are either in Him by faith or you are out of Him with your sins still upon you. If you are in Christ, then God sees you in Christ, and His righteousness is your righteousness. You stand complete in Him. "I in you"—is sanctification. That is Christian living down here. Is Christ living in you? Paul says, "I am crucified with Christ: nevertheless I live; yet not I, but Christ liveth in me: and the life which I now live in the flesh I live by the faith of the Son of God, who loved me, and gave himself for me" (Gal. 2:20).

He that hath my commandments, and keepeth them, he it is that loveth me: and he that loveth me shall be loved of my Father, and I will love him, and will manifest myself to him [John 14:21].

Don't say that you love Christ if you are not obeying Him. He is making this very clear here. Jesus is going to manifest Himself to the one who loves Him. Don't think this will be a manifestation by a vision. Later He says that it is the Holy Spirit who will take the things of Jesus and show them to you. Where does He do this? In the Scriptures. That is where Jesus is manifested.

Judas saith unto him, not Iscariot, Lord, how is it that

thou wilt manifest thyself unto us, and not unto the world? [John 14:22].

Judas is saying, "Lord, this is wonderful to be here and hear you say these things, but have you forgotten the world?" Here is the first missionary, by the way. The Lord Jesus answers him and His answer is the rest of the chapter.

> **Jesus answered and said unto him, If a man love me, he will keep my words: and my Father will love him, and we will come unto him, and make our abode with him.**

> **He that loveth me not keepeth not my sayings: and the word which ye hear is not mine, but the Father's which sent me [John 14:23-24].**

The way the world is going to find out about the Lord Jesus is through us, and obedience is imperative. Profession is not worth anything. Church membership is not really worth anything. The issue is our love for Him evidenced by our obedience. How about your love for Him? Does it discipline you? Is He real to you? These are the things that are important.

> **These things have I spoken unto you, being yet present with you.**

> **But the Comforter, which is the Holy Ghost, whom the Father will send in my name, he shall teach you all things, and bring all things to your remembrance, whatsoever I have said unto you [John 14:25-26].**

Jesus hasn't forgotten the world. In fact, He is thinking of the world. He has called these apostles into the Upper Room and has given them the truth so that they might take it to the world in the power of the Holy Spirit. The only way the truth can be given to the world is through these men. John was one of those men, and he has written this Gospel of John for us in the power of the Holy Spirit. Jesus assures them that the Holy Spirit will teach them all things and bring all things to their remembrance. It is evident that He did just that.

> Peace I leave with you, my peace I give unto you: not as the world giveth, give I unto you. Let not your heart be troubled, neither let it be afraid [John 14:27].

This verse takes us back to the beginning of this chapter. It is His final word of comfort. The peace He is talking about here is not the peace of sins forgiven. This is the glorious, wonderful peace that comes to the heart of those who are fully yielded to the Lord Jesus Christ. It is the peace of heart and mind of those who are in the will of God.

> Ye have heard how I said unto you, I go away, and come again unto you. If ye loved me, ye would rejoice, because I said, I go unto the Father: for my Father is greater than I.
>
> And now I have told you before it come to pass, that, when it is come to pass, ye might believe.
>
> Hereafter I will not talk much with you: for the prince of this world cometh, and hath nothing in me.
>
> But that the world may know that I love the Father; and as the Father gave me commandment, even so I do. Arise, let us go hence [John 14:28–31].

He tells them they should rejoice that He is going away because of the wonderful blessings that will come to them. Jesus Christ was going back to the Father and then He would send the Comforter to them.

He tells them He cannot walk and talk very much more with them, and He didn't—in a few hours He would be arrested and His disciples scattered. The prince of this world was coming. Jesus Christ would have another siege with Satan, which I believe took place in the Garden of Gethsemane. After that, He would go to the Cross for the sins of the world. After His ascension, the Comforter would come to indwell believers.

CHAPTER 15

THEME: Jesus is genuine Vine; disciples are branches

This fifteenth chapter is a part of the Upper Room Discourse, although our Lord probably did not speak it in the Upper Room. At least the assumption is that He did not, because the last statement in chapter 14 is, "Arise, let us go hence." Somewhere between the Upper Room and the Garden of Gethsemane our Lord spoke the words found in chapters 15 and 16, then prayed the prayer, recorded in chapter 17, as He entered the garden.

It has been the belief of many expositors that our Lord gave this chapter in a discourse down in the Valley of Kidron or on the side of the Mount of Olives, because we know that at that time there was a vineyard in that area which covered that valley. We also know that it was full moon because it was the time of the Passover. He may well have spoken these words as they walked through the vineyard. It would have been an appropriate place.

Another suggestion has been made by several English expositors—and it is the one I accept—that that night He went by the temple, following the Law as He so meticulously did. The gates would have been open during the Passover nights. Those beautiful gates of the temple were actually a tourist attraction. They had been forged in Greece, floated across the Hellespont, then brought to Jerusalem, and placed in Herod's temple there. The gates were made of bronze and wrought into them was a golden vine. That the vine symbolizes the nation Israel is apparent from the following verses: "Thou hast brought a vine out of Egypt: thou hast cast out the heathen, and planted it. Thou preparedst room before it, and didst cause it to take deep root, and it filled the land" (Ps. 80:8–9). "Now will I sing to my wellbeloved a song of my beloved touching his vineyard. My wellbeloved hath a vineyard in a very fruitful hill. . . . For the vineyard of the LORD of hosts is the house of Israel, and the men of Judah his pleasant plant: and he looked for judgment, but behold oppression; for righteousness, but behold a cry" (Isa. 5:1, 7). "Yet I had planted thee a noble vine, wholly a right seed: how then art thou turned into the degenerate plant of a strange vine unto me? (Jer. 2:21). "Israel is an empty vine, he bringeth forth fruit unto himself . . ." (Hos. 10:1). It is clear that the vine is a picture of the nation Israel.

Now, friend, our Lord is saying one of the most revolutionary things these men have ever heard. It sounds familiar to us today, but it was strange to their ears. Listen to Him.

JESUS IS GENUINE VINE; DISCIPLES ARE BRANCHES

I am the true vine, and my Father is the husbandman [John 15:1].

The word for true here is *alēthinos*, which means "genuine." A thing can be true as over against error and falsehood, or a thing can be true over against that which is a counterfeit. The latter is the way it is used here. We have had this word used in the same way previously in the Gospel of John. John the Baptist was a reflecting light, but Jesus Christ is the true Light. Moses gave bread in the wilderness, but Jesus Christ is the true Bread. So here Jesus is saying, "I am the true vine, the genuine vine."

These disciples had Jewish concepts and their thought patterns had been governed by the Old Testament. He is telling them now that the nation Israel is not the genuine vine. Their identification with the Jewish nation and the Jewish religion is not the essential thing. "I am the genuine vine." The important thing now is for the disciples to be related to Jesus Christ. That was revolutionary!

Our Lord used a marvelous figure of speech, and He made it very clear that it is not your identification with a religion or a ceremony or an organization that is essential. We are to be identified with Christ! We are in Christ by the baptism of the Holy Spirit the moment we trust Christ as our Savior and are born again as a child of God.

"My Father is the husbandman." This, too, is a startling word. In the Old Testament passages and in the parables, God is the owner of the vineyard. Here He is the keeper, the farmer, the One who takes care of the vineyard. Jesus is the genuine Vine, and the Father takes care of Him.

In the Old Testament it is prophesied that the Lord Jesus would grow up before Him as a tender plant and as a root out of the dry ground. Think how often the Father intervened to save Jesus from the Devil who wished to slay Him. The Father is the One who cared for the Vine, and He will care for the branches, too.

The branches must be joined to the Vine. For what purpose? For fruit-bearing. There are three words or phrases which are very important, and we will pick them up as we go along.

> **Every branch in me that beareth not fruit he taketh away: and every branch that beareth fruit, he purgeth it, that it may bring forth more fruit [John 15:2].**

"In me," that is, in Christ, is what it means to be saved. There are tremendous words like propitiation, reconciliation, and redemption that cover particular phases of salvation, but the entire spectrum of salvation is in the phrase "in Christ." There are only two groups of people: those who are in Christ and those who are not in Christ. How do you get "in Christ"? By the new birth. When you trust Christ as Savior, you become a child of God through faith. You are born again by the Spirit of God. The Holy Spirit does something else: He not only indwells you, but He also baptizes you. That is what puts every believer into the body of Christ—"every branch in me."

This passage is directed to believers, to those who are already in Christ. Jesus is not talking about *how* a person gets saved. He is not actually talking about salvation at all in this passage. Rather, He is talking about fruit-bearing, and that is the next word we wish to mark. Fruit is mentioned six times in the first ten verses. We will find as we go further that there are three degrees of fruit-bearing: fruit, more fruit, and much fruit. The whole theme here is fruit-bearing.

"Every branch in me that beareth not fruit he taketh away." Where does He take it? He takes it away from the place of fruit-bearing.

Listen how He describes this in verse 6. (We will come to verses 3–5 later.)

> **If a man abide not in me, he is cast forth as a branch, and is withered; and men gather them, and cast them into the fire, and they are burned [John 15:6].**

"Oh-oh," somebody says, "that sounds as if you lose your salvation." No, remember this passage is not talking about salvation but about fruit-bearing. It is talking about that which is the *result* of being saved.

First of all, what is the fruit? I do not believe that the fruit mentioned here refers to soul-winning, as so many people seem to think. I believe soul-winning is a by-product but not the fruit itself. The fruit is the fruit of the Spirit. "But the fruit of the Spirit is love, joy, peace, longsuffering, gentleness, goodness, faith, meekness, temperance. . ." (Gal. 5:22–23). This is fruit in the life of the believer. Abiding in Christ will produce effectual prayer, perpetual fruit, and celestial joy:

> **If ye abide in me, and my words abide in you, ye shall ask what ye will, and it shall be done unto you [John 15:7].**

That is prayer effectual.

> **Herein is my Father glorified, that ye bear much fruit; so shall ye be my disciples [John 15:8].**

This is fruit perpetual.

> **These things have I spoken unto you, that my joy might remain in you, and that your joy might be full [John 15:11].**

That is joy celestial.

If a person has such fruit in his life, he will be bringing men into the presence of God by his very life. That, of course, makes soul-winning a by-product.

"Every branch in me that beareth not fruit he taketh away." He wants fruit in our lives. If a branch does not bear fruit, how does He take it away? One of the ways He removes it is by taking such a person away from the place of fruit-bearing. I know many who have been set aside today because they were no longer effective for God. There are ministers like that and there are lay people like that. Removing such a branch does not mean they lose their salvation, but they are taken away from the place of fruit-bearing.

Sometimes this removing from the place of fruit-bearing is by death, physical death. I believe this is what John means in 1 John 5:16 when he says that there is a sin unto death. A Christian can go on sinning until God will remove him from the place of fruit-bearing by death. Ananias and Sapphira were removed by death from the early church, which was a holy church, a fruit-bearing church. These two liars could not stay in that church. I'm afraid they would be very comfortable in some of our churches today, but God would not permit them to remain in the early church.

"Every branch that beareth fruit, he purgeth it, that it may bring forth more fruit." The Greek word is *kathairō*, which means "to cleanse." Some people consider the purging to be pruning, and He does that too, but it really means to cleanse.

There is no doubt that the Lord does some pruning. He moves into our lives and takes out those things that offend, and sometimes it hurts. He removes things that are hindering us. I can speak to that subject and confess that it hurts. I think the Lord was pruning me when He permitted me to have a cancer and allowed it to stay in my body. He prunes out that which hinders our bearing fruit.

One of the reasons so many of God's children get hurt by this method of pruning is that they get so far from God, so far out of fellowship. The closer we are to God, the less it will hurt. I can remember playing hookey from school when I was a boy. We left our books at school and took off for the creek and went fishing. Although we didn't catch any fish, we had a lot of fun. We came in about the time school was out to get our books before going home so our parents wouldn't suspect that we had played hookey. The principal of the school figured we would do this, and when we walked into the room, he walked in right after us and said, "Boys, I'm glad to see you." We had to go to his office and wait while he got his switches. (We'd been through this before.) One of the fellows with me had been through this many times, and he gave me some of the best advice I've ever had. He said that when the principal started switching, we should move a step closer each time instead of backing off. The closer we were to him the less it would hurt. So the first time he hit me, instead of stepping back, I moved right in close to him, and I got so close I was where his fist was, and he wasn't hurting me at all. I have learned that is really good advice when the Lord chastens us also. Whom the Lord *loveth* he chasteneth. His chastening is not a sign that He is against us; He is trying to get fruit out of our lives. We tend to complain and move away from Him, but if we draw close to Him, it won't hurt nearly so much.

However, the "purging" in this verse literally means cleansing. When I was in the Bethlehem area, I saw that in their vineyards they let the grapevines grow on the ground, and they propped them up with a rock. Because the grapes get dirty and pests get on them, they actually go around and wash the grapes before they get ripe. So the Lord comes to our lives; He lifts us up and washes us so that we may bear more fruit. How does He do this?

Now ye are clean through the word which I have spoken unto you [John 15:3].

"Ye are clean through the word." The purging is accomplished by the Word of God. The cleansing power of the Word of God is a wonderful thing. We hear so much today about modern wash-day miracles, but I've never found them to be as miraculous as the claims made for them. The only true wash-day miracle is the cleansing power of the Word of God. "Seeing ye have purified your souls in obeying the truth through the Spirit unto unfeigned love of the brethren, see that ye love one another with a pure heart fervently: being born again, not of corruptible seed, but of incorruptible, by the word of God, which liveth and abideth for ever" (1 Pet. 1:22–23). We were born again by the

Word of God, washed from our sins. Then in our walk down here we get dirty and need the Word of God to cleanse us continually. That is one reason to study the Bible—to be cleansed. "Wherewithal shall a young man cleanse his way? by taking heed thereto according to thy word" (Ps. 119:9).

There are light views among believers today that you can live any kind of life so long as you are fundamental in your belief of salvation by the grace of God. Believe me, God uses the Word of God to reveal to us when we are not walking according to His will. The real test which reveals whether a person is genuine in his relationship to God is whether he is studying the Word of God and whether he is letting it have its way in his life! God intends for us to be obedient to His Word.

"Before I was afflicted I went astray: but now have I kept thy word" (Ps. 119:67). "It is good for me that I have been afflicted; that I might learn thy statutes" (Ps. 119:71). My friend, He uses affliction to bring us to the Word of God that you and I might be made serviceable to Him. I don't think that you will ever be clean before God if you don't study the Word of God. I believe that the people who are really dangerous are the ones who are as active as termites in our churches but who are reluctant to study the Word of God. I consider them the most dangerous element against the Word of God and the cause of Christ in this world. My friend, we need to study the Word of God and apply it to our lives.

> **Abide in me, and I in you. As the branch cannot bear fruit of itself, except it abide in the vine; no more can ye, except ye abide in me [John 15:4].**

We have come to the third word I want you to mark, which is *abide*. To abide in Christ means constant communion with Him all the time. We have just talked of the cleansing power of the Word of God. That is a part of abiding. We must be cleansed daily. There is a story about Spurgeon who stopped in the middle of the street, removed his hat, and prayed. One of his deacons saw this and asked him about it. Mr. Spurgeon said that a cloud had come between him and his Lord and he wanted to remove it immediately; he had stopped to confess his sinful thought. We need to confess our sins to the Lord to abide in Him, to stay in constant communion with Him.

Also to abide in Him, we are to keep His commandments.

> **If ye keep my commandments, ye shall abide in my love; even as I have kept my Father's commandments, and abide in his love.**
>
> **Ye are my friends, if ye do whatsoever I command you [John 15:10, 14].**

In our hymn books are songs like "Jesus Is a Friend of Mine" and "There's not a Friend like the Lowly Jesus." Friend, let me say this kindly. There is no lowly Jesus today but a glorified Christ at God's right hand. Calling Jesus a friend of mine is sentimental and really wrong. If I would say that the President of the United States is my friend, I bring him down to my level. If he says that I am his friend, that is wonderful. Listen to what Jesus says. "Ye are my friend, if ye do whatsoever I command you." We don't need all this sentimental trash today. We need some honest heart-searching. Are we doing what Jesus has commanded us to do? Obedience is essential to abiding.

> **As the Father hath loved me, so have I loved you: continue ye in my love [John 15:9].**

Abiding is a continuing communion. That is the relationship of branch and vine. I have a 72' x 123' ranch here in California on which grow four avocado trees, three orange trees, and one tangerine tree. I have never had to say to the branches that they should abide in the tree or we wouldn't have any fruit. I've never been up in the night to inspect them or come home unexpectedly and found the branches running around away from the tree. They abide and they bear fruit. You think I am being ridiculous. However, many Christians think they can live like the Devil all week and on Saturday night, then come in and serve the Lord on Sunday. I happen to know because I tried that for years. My friend, we must be in constant communion with Him to bear fruit. That means when you wake in the morning, when you are at your desk in the office, when you are driving your car on the streets, you are abiding in constant communion.

> **I am the vine, ye are the branches: He that abideth in me, and I in him, the same bringeth forth much fruit: for without me ye can do nothing [John 15:5].**

Because we have free will, we can break fellowship with God by allowing sin in our life, by stepping out of the will of God, or by worldliness. He wants us to abide so that we bring forth much fruit. You will notice here that there is a similarity to the parable of the sower. Remember that some of the seed fell on good ground and brought forth thirtyfold—that is fruit. Some of the seed brought forth sixty—that is more fruit. Some of the seed brought forth an hundredfold—that is much fruit. God wants us to bear much fruit.

> **If a man abide not in me, he is cast forth as a branch, and is withered; and men gather them, and cast them into the fire, and they are burned [John 15:6].**

Let me say again that this is talking about our fruit-bearing, the product of our salvation. It is not talking about how we are to be saved. Paul uses another illustration for this same thing: "For other foundation can no man lay than that is laid, which is Jesus Christ. Now if any man build upon this foundation gold, silver, precious stones, wood, hay, stubble; every man's work shall be made manifest: for the day shall declare it, because it shall be revealed by fire; and the fire shall try every man's work of what sort it is." (This is talking about the works of the believers, the fruit in the life of a believer. Fire will purify gold and silver and precious stones and draw off the dross. Wood, hay, and stubble will go up in smoke. That is the same as our verse which says the works will be cast into the fire and burned.) "If any man's work abide which he hath built thereupon, he shall receive a reward" (1 Cor. 3:11–14). I believe that rewards will be given only for the fruit in our lives—and we don't produce the fruit; He produces the fruit when we abide in Him.

A branch that is not abiding in Christ "is cast forth as a branch, and is withered; and men gather them, and cast them into the fire, and they are burned." This is amplified by 1 Corinthians 3:15: "If any man's work shall be burned, he shall suffer loss: but he himself shall be saved; yet so as by fire." He may get to heaven smelling as if he had been bought at a fire sale, but he will not lose his salvation.

One of the saddest things is that today the average Christian believes that normal Christian living is failure. They think that bearing much fruit is entirely out of the question and are willing to live on a low plane hoping to produce just a little fruit. Remember that the Lord wants us to produce much fruit.

> If ye abide in me, and my words abide in you, ye shall ask what ye will, and it shall be done unto you.
>
> Herein is my Father glorified, that ye bear much fruit; so shall ye be my disciples [John 15:7–8].

This is a marvelous prayer promise, but notice the condition. "If ye abide in me, and my words abide in you" means to be obedient to Him. Then we will have effectual prayer. The whole purpose of the abiding and of the praying is that the Father may have glory. This eliminates prayer for selfish reasons. The issue is fruit-bearing. God is glorified when we do bear fruit.

> As the Father hath loved me, so have I loved you: continue ye in my love.
>
> If ye keep my commandments, ye shall abide in my love; even as I have kept my Father's commandments, and abide in his love.
>
> These things have I spoken unto you, that my joy might remain in you, and that your joy might be full [John 15:9–11].

The Lord wants us to have a good time. One of the fruits of the Spirit is to have joy in your life. I am mortally afraid of super-pious Christians who have no humor in their lives, yet walk around with a Bible under their arms. A fruit-bearing Christian will have a lot of fun in this life. There will be fun in going to a Bible study; there will be fun in serving the Lord. A life in fellowship with Christ is a joyous life.

> **This is my commandment, That ye love one another, as I have loved you [John 15:12].**

Remember He is talking to believers in this discourse. We are to love each other as He has loved us! It is sad to see Christians in our churches who tear down each other and gossip about one another. The Spirit of God is not working in such a situation. One can have Bible teaching and still reject this commandment of our Lord. To love as He has loved us is putting it on a very high plane. Only the Spirit of God can produce such love in our lives.

> **Greater love hath no man than this, that a man lay down his life for his friends [John 15:13].**

There is the test.

> **Ye are my friends, if ye do whatsoever I command you [John 15:14].**

The Christian life is not a hit-and-miss proposition. The Christian life is following His instructions, and the instructions are clear. If you follow these instructions, you will bear fruit. He laid down His life for us; He asks us to obey Him. He is our friend because He died for us. We are His friends when we keep His commandments.

He doesn't ask all of us to die for Him. Someone once asked Dwight L. Moody whether he had "dying grace." Mr. Moody replied that he didn't have it, but when He needed it, the Lord would give it to him. And He did.

Henceforth I call you not servants; for the servant knoweth not what his lord doeth: but I have called you friends; for all things that I have heard of my Father I have made known unto you.

Ye have not chosen me, but I have chosen you, and ordained you, that ye should go and bring forth fruit, and that your fruit should remain: that whatsoever ye shall ask of the Father in my name, he may give it you [John 15:15–16].

We are the friends of Jesus if we do whatsoever He has commanded us. Now He tells us that He has opened up His heart to us. God wants to reveal Himself to us. Remember how He searched out Abraham to reveal His plan to him because Abraham was His friend. Now Jesus tells us that He has revealed the things of God to us. That is what a friend does. How many people can you go to and open up your heart? One of the things that should characterize a believer is that you could go to him and tell him your problems and get understanding and help and encouragement from him. This is how we are to love one another.

Now, notice, "Ye have not chosen me, but I have chosen you." A great many people do not like the doctrine of election, but it is wonderful and practical. Many a discouraged Christian has cast himself on the Lord saying, "Lord, you called me and chose me and I'm your child." Dr. G. Campbell Morgan said, "He chose me; therefore I am His responsibility." That is trust!

This little crowd of disciples is going to scatter in a few hours. The Shepherd will be crucified, and the sheep will scatter. At such an hour Jesus tells them, "Ye have not chosen me, but I have chosen you."

A preacher, who had been converted late in life, had been guilty of stealing before he was saved. After he had just started preaching about His Savior and was still a new Christian, he passed a hen house on his way home from church one night. It was a great temptation for him, but he stopped and prayed, "Lord, your property is in danger, and I don't mean the chickens." It is wonderful to call upon the Lord like that.

His great purpose is that we should produce fruit, not just passing fruit, but fruit that will remain. It must all be in His will. If we abide in Him, then we can ask in His name. Answers to our prayers are a pretty good barometer of our spirituality.

He climaxes this section on fruit-bearing by mentioning again that we should love one another.

> **These things I command you, that ye love one another [John 15:17].**

This should be the relationship of believers. There is also a relationship with the world, and now He goes into that subject.

> **If the world hate you, ye know that it hated me before it hated you.**
>
> **If ye were of the world, the world would love his own: but because ye are not of the world, but I have chosen you out of the world, therefore the world hateth you [John 15:18–19].**

Notice what will happen if you are a child of God. The world will hate you. I believe that a Christian's popularity can be an indication of how he is representing Christ to the world. I do not believe a Christian can be popular in the world. No Christian has any right to be more popular than Jesus was. Beware of a compromising position in order to be popular. The world will not love a real child of God. The world will love you if you are of the world. You don't have to act oddly or be superpious. The world will hate you if you are a child of God. This is difficult, especially for young people who want so much to be popular. Let's tell our young people what the Lord says. They are not going to be popular with the world if they are the children of God.

Unfortunately, there are folk in the church today who are not honestly born-again, and they will also hate you if you are a child of God. They will hate the preacher if he is true to the Word of God. May I say again, beware of the Christian who is popular with the world.

Remember the word that I said unto you, The servant is not greater than his lord. If they have persecuted me, they will also persecute you; if they have kept my saying, they will keep yours also.

But all these things will they do unto you for my name's sake, because they know not him that sent me.

If I had not come and spoken unto them, they had not had sin: but now they have no cloak for their sin [John 15:20–22].

Don't try to be greater than your Lord. The servant should not be more popular than the Master. Just keep giving out the Word. Those who persecute have two problems: they do not know the Father, and they do not want their sins revealed. Jesus Christ turned the light of heaven upon the souls of men. Whenever one turns on a light, things begin to happen. The rats and snakes and bugs and lizards hate the light and they all run for cover. They will hate the one who turns on the light, too, by the way. Jesus says, "They hated me without a cause." There is no cause for hate in Jesus. The cause is in the sinful hearts of men.

He that hateth me hateth my Father also [John 15:23].

This is an important verse. The world does not hate their idea of God, as some vague Someone out yonder. It is Christ they hate. Jesus says when a man hates Him, he is hating God the Father also. You can say you believe in God and be popular. The real test is your relationship and attitude toward Jesus Christ. You cannot be popular and believe in the Lord Jesus Christ, because He is the One who is hated.

If I had not done among them the works which none other man did, they had not had sin: but now have they both seen and hated both me and my Father.

But this cometh to pass, that the word might be fulfilled that is written in their law, They hated me without a cause [John 15:24–25].

Some wag has said, "God created man in His image and now man is creating God in his image." That is the kind of God they want today and the kind of God they think is running the universe. Jesus quotes this as a fulfillment of Psalms 35:19 and 69:4 when He says they hated Him without a cause. They hate Jesus Christ because they have created a false god who is not the God of the Bible.

> But when the Comforter is come, whom I will send unto you from the Father, even the Spirit of truth, which proceedeth from the Father, he shall testify of me:
>
> And ye also shall bear witness, because ye have been with me from the beginning [John 15:26–27].

The Holy Spirit bears testimony concerning Christ. If the Lord Jesus Christ is real to you, that is the work of the Holy Spirit. One way to tell whether the Spirit of God is working is whether Christ is being glorified. If the Lord Jesus is not as real to you as you wish He were, ask the Spirit of God to do a work in your heart. We need the reality of Christ in our hearts and lives.

Jesus told these men that they would bear witness to Him, and they certainly did that. It is the witness of John concerning the Lord Jesus Christ that we are studying right now. No one but the apostles could bear such a witness because they had been with Jesus from the beginning.

CHAPTER 16

THEME: Jesus will send Holy Spirit during His absence

This chapter concludes the Upper Room Discourse. We learned in the preceding chapter that His own should love one another. This is a real rebuke to us. It is a rebuke that He must command us to do that. It is a rebuke because it shows that we are not nearly as attractive as we think we are. We need help supernaturally to enable us to love one another. Then He told us that we are to identify with Him which will cause the world to hate us.

Also He told His disciples that if He had not come, they would not have known sin. He did not mean that they did not have their own sins but, that since He had come, their personal sins were as nothing compared to the immeasurable guilt of rejecting the Savior of the world and the Lord of glory.

There are not only degrees of rewards in heaven, but there are degrees of punishment in hell. The person today who hears about Jesus Christ and turns his back on Him is in the same category as Judas Iscariot who in the presence of Christ turned his back upon Him. To reject Him is the greatest sin of all. Jesus warns them about this in the coming chapter.

JESUS WILL SEND HOLY SPIRIT
DURING HIS ABSENCE

The chapter begins with Jesus still talking about the hatred of the world.

> These things have I spoken unto you, that ye should not be offended [John 16:1].

What things? The things mentioned in chapter 15.

> **They shall put you out of the synagogues: yea, the time cometh, that whosoever killeth you will think that he doeth God service.**
>
> **And these things will they do unto you, because they have not known the Father, nor me [John 16:2-3].**

The Lord didn't want the apostles to be offended, that is, *scandalized* at what would happen to them. It is characteristic of founders of organizations, and especially of religions, to attempt to present a glorious future for their organizations. The method of the world is to build up the wonderful benefits and to play down the hardships and disadvantages and privations and sacrifices. How different our Lord is!

While it is true that in chapter 14 our Lord told us that He is going to prepare a place for us and that He will receive us unto Himself, He also makes it very clear that if we are going to follow Him down here, it means to forsake all. He said that foxes have holes and birds have nests, but He didn't have a place to lay His head. He said that if we are going to follow Him, we must take up our cross—not *His* Cross—our own cross, and follow Him. If we suffer with Him down here, we shall reign with Him up there. He was despised and rejected. He was a Man of Sorrows and acquainted with grief. He said His followers are going to be *in* the world but not *of* the world and that the world will hate them. He made all of that very clear. He never said that it would be easy for His followers down here.

The professing church, instead of taking the position of Christ, has gone out into the world, boasting that they are going to convert the world. They, of course, haven't done it in over nineteen hundred years. In their attempt they always try to popularize religion, make it very attractive to the world. You will find that today there are churches using all kinds of devices to attract the ungodly. Today music has come down to the level of the world. They say, "We have to do this to win the world." Who told them they were going to win the world? I'm not talking about liberal churches now—they went off the track years ago—I am talking about fundamental churches. Today fundamental churches are going off the track. In them you will find *enemies* of the

Word of God! Although they wouldn't dare attack the Bible, they level their attack against the man who is preaching the Word of God.

There are tragic stories everywhere. I know a deacon in a church who has already destroyed three preachers. One man left broken in health, another simply left the ministry, and the third resigned. I know a minister who is selling second-hand cars. He says he would rather deal with second-hand cars than with second-hand Christians. Friend, if you stand for the Word of God, you will find that the world won't love you. You will experience the hatred that Christ experienced. "These things have I spoken unto you, that ye should not be offended." He is warning them ahead of time in order to strengthen them and let them know what is coming. He loves them right on through to the very end, and He lets them know that He will be with them and that He understands what they are going through.

He knew they would have moments when they would be offended because of Him. He knew that Peter would deny Him that very night. He told His disciples what would happen in order to encourage them and to let them know that He would sustain them through it all. He forewarned them to establish their responsibility to God.

"They shall put you out of the synagogues" means excommunication.

In that day to be excommunicated was the worst that could happen to a religious Jew. It would cost these men to stand for the Lord Jesus Christ. The religious Jews would cast them out. My friend, I'm very candid to say again that if you are standing for Christ, it is going to cost you something.

Jesus again traces the source of the hatred. Because they do not know the Father, they do not know the Lord Jesus Christ. Also this is why the world hates the Word of God. This is why the world hates the genuine believer.

> **But these things have I told you, that when the time shall come, ye may remember that I told you of them. And these things I said not unto you at the beginning, because I was with you [John 16:4].**

He is letting them know what is coming and He is training them for what is to come. The Lord always prepares us, friend. During my years of being a pastor, I have learned that this is God's method. I have learned in my own experience and by watching others that the Lord trains and prepares us for that which lies ahead.

> **But now I go my way to him that sent me; and none of you asketh me, Whither goest thou? [John 16:5].**

It is true that Simon Peter had asked Him where He was going, but Peter had asked the question of a little child. He is saying that none of them has really discerned what is going to take place. None of them has asked intelligently, with spiritual perception.

> **But because I have said these things unto you, sorrow hath filled your heart [John 16:6].**

These men were letting the fact that He was going to leave them absolutely overwhelm them with sorrow. Friend, that is something which Christians today need to avoid. Many Christians let one experience embitter them. They experience some disappointment in an individual or in a church and are overwhelmed by sorrow and turn from God. Some people won't darken the door of a church because they are bitter over some incident in the past. Others who have lost loved ones remain constantly in mourning. This is not the way it should be. We are not to be overcome by sorrow.

> **Nevertheless I tell you the truth; It is expedient for you that I go away: for if I go not away, the Comforter will not come unto you; but if I depart, I will send him unto you [John 16:7].**

"It is expedient for you that I go away"—in other words, it is better for you. Why was it best for the Lord Jesus to leave? I can suggest several reasons and I'm sure you can think of more. One of the reasons is this: His purpose in coming to this world was to die—". . . the Son of man came not to be ministered unto, but to minister, and to give his life a ransom for many" (Mark 10:45). When this was accomplished, He went back to the Father because He had finished the work He was sent to do. Then, there is another reason: when He came to this earth, He took upon Himself our humanity. God is omnipresent, but Jesus limited Himself by becoming a man. That means that, when He was in Galilee, He could not be down in Bethany. Remember that Mary and Martha reminded Him of that when they said that, if He had been there, their brother would not have died. In other words, if the Lord Jesus were in the world today in His human body, He couldn't be here where I am and with you where you are at the same time.

Therefore, He tells them He will send the Holy Spirit to them. The Holy Spirit will be in all places. He is right with me today and He is with you today. Jesus says this is better. He will send the Comforter, the Paraclete, and He will come to us and dwell in us.

When the Holy Spirit comes, He will perform several ministries, one of which He mentions here:

> **And when he is come, he will reprove the world of sin, and of righteousness, and of judgment:**
>
> **Of sin, because they believe not on me;**
>
> **Of righteousness, because I go to my Father, and ye see me no more;**
>
> **Of judgment, because the prince of this world is judged [John 16:8–11].**

The Greek word for "reprove" is elegchō which means "to convict." I counted that word used in "The Trial of Socrates," as recorded by Plato, and found it twenty-three times. It is a legal term. When the Holy Spirit is come, He will convict the world in the way a judge or a prosecuting attorney presents evidence to bring a conviction. The Spirit of God wants to present evidence in your heart and in my heart to bring us to a place of conviction, and that, of course, means a place of decision. There must be a conviction before we can turn in faith and trust to Jesus Christ.

In the present ministry of the Holy Spirit in the world, He will convict the world of three things: sin, righteousness, and judgment. Our Lord explains for us what that sin means. "Sin, because they believe not on me." What is the greatest sin in all the world? Murder? No. Who are the greatest sinners in this age? We've had some rascals, haven't we? Every age has had rascals. We might point out Hitler, or Stalin, or Karl Marx, or the Mafia. Well, who is the greatest sinner today? I want to say to you very carefully that you could be the greatest sinner living today. You may say, "Now wait a minute, preacher, you can't say that about me! I'm no rascal; I'm a law-abiding citizen." The question is this: Have you accepted Christ? Unbelief is a state and there is no remedy if you refuse to trust Christ. "Of sin, because they believe not on me." If you do not trust Him, you are lost. It is just as simple as that. It is just as important as that. This is a decision that every man must make. The man today, whoever he is, if he is rejecting Jesus Christ, is, in the sight of God, the greatest sinner. Remember that Jesus said, "If I had not come and spoken unto them, they had not had sin: but now they have no cloak for their sin" (John 15:22). Everyone who has ever heard the gospel is responsible for his decision concerning Jesus Christ. To reject Christ is sin.

Secondly, He will convict the world of righteousness. Jesus Christ was delivered for our offenses and was raised again for our justification (see Rom. 4:25). Jesus Christ returned to the Father because He had completed His work here. When He died on the Cross, He died a judgment death. He took my guilt and your guilt and He died in our place. He was delivered for our offenses. But He was raised for our justification. He was raised from the dead that you and I might not only have our sins subtracted, but so that we might have His righteousness added. That is very important because you and I need righteousness. It is not enough to have our sins forgiven. We cannot stand in God's presence if we are nothing more than pardoned criminals. Christ has made over to us *His* righteousness. That is the righteousness Paul spoke of: ". . . that I may win Christ, and be found in him, not having mine own righteousness, which is of the law, but that which is through the faith of Christ, the righteousness which is of God by faith" (Phil. 3:8–9). He not only subtracts our sin, but He adds His righteousness. If we are to have any standing before God, we must be in Christ and He is our righteousness. Either we have as much right in heaven as Christ Himself has, or we have no right there at all. He was delivered for our offenses, and He was raised again for our justification (righteousness).

Thirdly, He convicts the world of judgment. Does this mean that judgment is coming some day? No, not in this verse. "Of judgment, because the prince of this world is judged." The prince of this world, Satan, has already been judged. It is difficult for a great many believers to understand that we live in a judged world. One hears people say that they'll take their chances. They act as if they are on trial. My friend, you are not on trial. God has already declared you a lost sinner, and He has already judged you—"For the wages of sin is death; but the gift of God is eternal life through Jesus Christ our Lord" (Rom. 6:23). We live in a world that has already been judged and is like the man waiting in death row for his execution. The judgment against all of us is "Guilty" because all our own righteousnesses are as filthy rags in the sight of God. If we had to stand before God in our own filthy rags, we would not only be ashamed of ourselves, but we would also see how guilty we are.

Remember that Paul reasoned with old Felix concerning judgment to come. That frightened him. Today many people don't like to hear about judgment, and they resent it a great deal. The lost world hates many things about God: for instance, His omnipotence. They don't like the fact that it is His universe and He is running it His way. They don't like it that God saves by grace and that man has already been declared lost. These are the three things of which the Holy Spirit convicts the world today.

I have yet many things to say unto you, but ye cannot bear them now.

Howbeit when he, the Spirit of truth, is come, he will guide you into all truth: for he shall not speak of himself; but whatsoever he shall hear, that shall he speak: and he will shew you things to come.

He shall glorify me: for he shall receive of mine, and shall shew it unto you [John 16:12–14].

We don't know it all. We are to keep growing in grace and in the knowledge of Him. How can we do it? Just reading the Bible is not the complete answer; the Holy Spirit must be our Teacher as we read.

The Spirit of God is the Spirit of Truth. He will lead and guide you into all truth. He guided the apostles just as the Lord said He would, and we find these truths in the Epistles. The Spirit of God came to these men at Pentecost, and He guided them in the truth both in their preaching and in their writing.

We can see how this was fulfilled in the apostles. The ministry of the Holy Spirit has been to complete the teaching of the Lord Jesus Christ. The Epistles glorify Christ and show Him as the Head of the church. They speak of His coming again to establish His Kingdom. The Epistles are the unfolding of the person and ministry of Christ. They also tell of things to come and certainly the Book of Revelation does this.

Notice the seven steps that are here: (1) The Holy Spirit, the Spirit of Truth, has come; (2) He will guide you into all truth; (3) He will not speak of Himself; (4) He shall speak whatsoever He shall hear; (5) He will show you things to come; (6) He shall glorify Jesus; and (7) He shall receive of mine and show it unto you.

Since we have been told these steps, we have a way of testing what we hear and read. I listened to a man on a radio program saying, "We are having a Holy Ghost revival; the Holy Ghost is working: the Holy Ghost is doing this and that." The minute he said all those things, I knew the Holy Ghost was not working. Why? Because the Lord Jesus made it very clear that the Holy Ghost will not speak of Himself. Then how can you tell when the Holy Spirit is working? He will glorify Christ. My friend, when in a meeting or a Bible study you suddenly get a glimpse of the Lord Jesus and He becomes wonderful, very real, and meaningful to you, that is the working of the Holy Spirit. Jesus said, "He shall glorify me."

> **All things that the Father hath are mine: therefore said I, that he shall take of mine, and shall shew it unto you [John 16:15].**

Again the Lord Jesus is making Himself equal with God. Whatever the Father has, Jesus has. "He shall take of mine" means He will take the things of God and show them unto us. Only He can do that. ". . . Eye hath not seen, nor ear heard, neither have entered into the heart of man, the things which God hath prepared for them that love him. But God hath revealed them unto us by his Spirit . . ." (1 Cor. 2:9–10). The Spirit is the One who searches the deep things of God and He alone can show these things to us.

> **A little while, and ye shall not see me: and again, a little while, and ye shall see me, because I go to the Father [John 16:16].**

What did He mean? He meant that He would be arrested, and they would be scattered like sheep and separated from Him. He'd be crucified and buried. He would be absent a little while and they wouldn't see Him. On the third day He would come back, and so in a little while they would see Him. This has a fuller, richer, deeper meaning for us today.

> **Then said some of his disciples among themselves, What is this that he saith unto us, A little while, and ye shall not see me: and again, a little while, and ye shall see me: and, Because I go to the Father?**

> **They said therefore, What is this that he saith, A little while? we cannot tell what he saith.**

> **Now Jesus knew that they were desirous to ask him, and said unto them, Do ye inquire among yourselves of that I said, A little while, and ye shall not see me: and again, a little while, and ye shall see me?**

Verily, verily, I say unto you, That ye shall weep and lament, but the world shall rejoice: and ye shall be sorrowful, but your sorrow shall be turned into joy [John 16:17-20].

They didn't know exactly what He meant. There was to be the little while that He was in the grave—that was three days. Then there was to come another "little while" because He would go to the Father (which has been over nineteen hundred years now). He promised not to leave them comfortless, not to leave them orphans. He would be with them in the person of the Holy Spirit. He would take the things of Christ and make them real to them. That is where you and I live today. During these nineteen hundred years the Spirit of God has made Him real to multitudes. They have gone through sorrow; they have known what it is to be hated and to be ridiculed. He has brought them through that. Our sorrow shall be turned into joy.

A woman when she is in travail hath sorrow, because her hour is come: but as soon as she is delivered of the child, she remembereth no more the anguish, for joy that a man is born into the world.

And ye now therefore have sorrow: but I will see you again, and your heart shall rejoice, and your joy no man taketh from you [John 16:21-22].

Regardless of where you are or who you are, if you have accepted Jesus, my friend, you are a child of God. If you are in sorrow and there are tears in your eyes, if you have a broken heart, be assured that joy cometh in the morning. He is going to bring joy into your life. I think that when we get in His presence and look back on this life, if we have any regrets, it will be because we didn't suffer more for Him. The joy of His presence will overwhelm any sorrow we may have down here.

And in that day ye shall ask me nothing. Verily, verily, I say unto you, Whatsoever ye shall ask the Father in my name, he will give it you.

Hitherto have ye asked nothing in my name: ask, and ye shall receive, that your joy may be full [John 16:23–24].

This is the third time He speaks of praying in His name. We have already seen that "praying in my name" refers to one who is abiding in Him, obeying Him. You cannot simply tag His name on to the end of a request and expect to get what you ask. That is not what He is saying.

Remember that these disciples had never prayed to the Father in the name of Jesus. You and I today are to pray *to* God the Father *in* Jesus' name. Someone may ask whether we can't pray to Jesus. I think you can if you wish to, but why do you rob yourself of an intercessor? Jesus is up there at God's right hand for you, praying for you. That is the reason that we should pray to the Father in the name of Jesus.

These things have I spoken unto you in proverbs: but the time cometh, when I shall no more speak unto you in proverbs, but I shall shew you plainly of the Father.

At that day ye shall ask in my name: and I say not unto you, that I will pray the Father for you:

For the Father himself loveth you, because ye have loved me, and have believed that I came out from God [John 16:25–27].

"The time cometh"—He is nearing His crucifixion, the hour of redemption for which He has come into the world. After that, they are to ask the Father in Jesus' name. He is trying to teach them that the Father is not a hard taskmaster who is reluctant to answer prayer. He is saying in effect, "If you think that I have to ask the Father to be good to you and to be generous to you, you are wrong. The Father Himself loveth you. I don't have to ask Him to love you. He loves you already. The Father isn't hard to get along with. He loves you and that is the reason He will answer your prayer that you pray in My name."

Today God wants to hear and answer prayers, but they must come from the heart of one who loves Christ, and is in fellowship with Him, obeying Him.

I came forth from the Father, and am come into the world: again, I leave the world, and go to the Father [John 16:28].

It is generally conceded that the key verse to the Gospel of John is John 20:30–31, but I would like to put beside it this verse. The eternal Son came into the world for one purpose: to redeem man. When the mission was accomplished, He returned to the Father. This is the movement in the Gospel of John. He has painted a black picture of coming persecution but concludes the chapter with victory.

This verse is bigger than Bethlehem; it is wider than space. It reaches back into eternity, beyond the boundaries of space to the throne of God. Then it speaks of those few moments He spent on this earth. He came in out of eternity; He went back into eternity.

His disciples said unto him, Lo, now speakest thou plainly, and speakest no proverb.

Now are we sure that thou knowest all things, and needest not that any man should ask thee: by this we believe that thou camest forth from God [John 16:29–30].

It should be plain for us to understand that the Lord Jesus is God manifest in the flesh. There is this great conviction coming over the disciples. They are convinced of the facts. They have seen that He has come forth from the Father and that He has come into the world. He is the Messiah; He is the Savior He claims to be. However, they still do not understand the dark waters of death through which He must pass, nor the door of resurrection and ascension back into the Father's glory. They still don't quite comprehend it. But after nineteen hundred years do we comprehend it?

Jesus answered them, Do ye now believe?

Behold, the hour cometh, yea, is now come, that ye shall be scattered, every man to his own, and shall leave me

alone: and yet I am not alone, because the Father is with me [John 16:31–32].

The hour was coming when these men would all scatter. They would leave Him alone; and yet He was not alone "because the Father is with me." That is one of the great mysteries. God was in Christ reconciling the world to Himself (see 2 Cor. 5:19). That is a great truth, and it is also equally true that on the Cross Jesus cried out, ". . . My God, my God, why hast thou forsaken me?" (Mark 15:34), which is a quotation from Psalm 22. The explanation is, "But thou art holy, O thou that inhabitest the praises of Israel" (Ps. 22:3). Jesus Christ was made sin for us, friend. There was a rent in the Godhead as well as a rent in the veil. Yet at that very moment, God was in Christ reconciling the world unto Himself.

This is a mystery that the human mind cannot understand. Friends, we do not have enough brains to comprehend the redemption that He wrought on the Cross. No wonder God wrapped the mantle of night around that Cross as if to say, "You will never be able to enter into what is happening here." I believe that throughout the endless ages of eternity you and I will continually understand something new and wonderful about the death of the Lord Jesus for us. It will cause us to get down on our faces before Him afresh and anew.

These things I have spoken unto you, that in me ye might have peace. In the world ye shall have tribulation: but be of good cheer; I have overcome the world [John 16:33].

Peace. He closes with peace. The child of God can have peace in this life because peace is found in Christ and in no other place. You won't find peace in the church. You won't find peace in Christian service. Peace is found in the person of Jesus Christ.

"In the world ye shall have tribulation." Our Lord made that very clear. There is no peace in the world, only trouble. He was right, wasn't He? But He has overcome the world! His victory is our victory.

I hear so much today about the victorious life. The only One who ever lived a victorious life was Christ. You and I cannot live it. We can let Him live it in us—that is all. When you and I learn to identify ourselves with Him and come into close fellowship with Him, then we will begin to experience the peace of God in our hearts. Also we will be of good cheer. There is trouble in the world but in our lives there will be joy. Peace and joy! How important they are. "These things I have spoken unto you, that in me ye might have peace. In the world ye shall have tribulation: but be of good cheer; I have overcome the world."

CHAPTER 17

THEME: *The Lord's Prayer—Jesus prays for Himself; Jesus prays for disciples; Jesus prays for His church*

We now come to one of the most remarkable chapters in the Bible. It is the longest prayer in the Bible, although it would take you only three minutes to read it. I think that is a good indication of the length of public prayers. If you can't say all you've got to say in three minutes, then you've got too much to say. I'll be very frank with you. I think brief prayers, thought out right to the point, are more effective than these long, rambling ones we hear. No wonder prayer meetings are as dead as a dodo bird!

The Upper Room Discourse is like climbing a staircase or like climbing a mountain, climaxing in this prayer. I would like to quote to you what others have said about this great chapter.

Matthew Henry: "It is the most remarkable prayer following the most full and consoling discourse ever uttered on the earth."

Martin Luther: "This is truly beyond measure a warm and hearty prayer. He opens the depths of His heart, both in reference to us and to His Father, and He pours them all out. It sounds so honest, so simple. It is so deep, so rich, so wide. No one can fathom it."

Philip Melanchthon, another of the reformers: "There is no voice which has ever been heard, either in heaven or in earth, more exalted, more holy, more fruitful, more sublime than the prayer offered up by the Son to God Himself."

This is the prayer which John Knox read over and over in his lifetime. When he was on his deathbed, his wife asked him. "Where do you want me to read?" He replied, "Read where I first put my anchor down, in the seventeenth chapter of John." We have the record of many others who have read it over and over. Dr. Fisher, who was bishop of Rochester under Henry VIII, had this read as the last portion of Scripture just before his martyrdom.

This is a great portion of Scripture. I feel wholly and totally inadequate to deal with this prayer. It is His high priestly intercession for us. It is a revelation to us of the communication which, I think, constantly passes between the Lord Jesus and the Father in heaven. His entire life was a life of prayer. He began His ministry by going into a solitary place to pray. Often He went up into a mountain to pray and spent the night in prayer. He is our great Intercessor. He prays for you and for me. If you forgot to pray this morning, He didn't. He prayed for you this morning.

God always hears and answers Jesus' prayer just the way He prays it. God answered my prayer also, but not always the way I pray it—sometimes He must answer my prayer with a no, or He may accomplish what I ask by a completely different method or at a different time. However, Jesus said, "Father, I thank thee that thou hast heard me. And I knew that thou hearest me always: but because of the people which stand by I said it, that they may believe that thou hast sent me" (John 11:41–42).

THE LORD'S PRAYER—JESUS PRAYS FOR HIMSELF

I want you to notice that it is not out of line nor even a mark of selfishness to pray for one's self. I believe that when you and I go to God in prayer, we need to get our own hearts and lives right with God. We need to get in tune with heaven, as it were. Every instrument should be tuned up before it is played. Before you and I begin to pray for others, we need to pray for ourselves. That is not selfishness; it is essential.

These words spake Jesus, and lifted up his eyes to heaven, and said, Father, the hour is come; glorify thy Son, that thy Son also may glorify thee [John 17:1].

"These words spake Jesus." Which words? The chapters we have just read, chapters 13—16. Now He stops speaking to the disciples, and He speaks to the Father. Although He is speaking to the Father in this chapter, He is speaking to Him for their benefit—and for our benefit also. He is our great Intercessor today. We may wonder what He is praying for. Well, here it is. This is the Lord's Prayer, the prayer that He prays to the Father.

The prayer in the Sermon on the Mount is not really the Lord's Prayer. It is the prayer that He taught to the disciples. When Jesus begins with "Our Father," He means this for all the believers. However, Jesus calls God "Father" in a different sense. After His resurrection He said to Mary, "I am not yet ascended to my Father: but go to my brethren, and say unto them, I ascend unto my Father, and your Father; and to my God, and your God" (John 20:17). In other words, "I have not yet ascended to your Father, yours by the new birth, and to My Father, Mine because of My position in the Trinity." Also, it could never be the prayer of Jesus to say, "Forgive us our debts, our sins." He never had any sins. He could not pray that prayer. By the same token, you and I can never pray this prayer of John 17. This is His prayer.

Apparently our Lord prayed this prayer as He was walking along. It says that He "lifted up his eyes to heaven," which means that His eyes were open. Of course we can pray without bowing our heads and closing our eyes. We can pray as we walk or as we work or as we drive.

Now notice His prayer. It begins, "Father, the hour is come." What hour? Well, the hour that had been set back yonder in eternity. As He speaks, the clock is striking the hour that was set way back in eternity, because He was the Lamb of God slain before the foundation of the world. It was arranged back there; now "the hour is come." Remember that when He began His ministry at the wedding of Cana, His mother said to Him, "They have no wine." His answer to her was, "Woman, what have I to do with thee? mine hour is not yet come" (John 2:3–4). Now the hour has come, the hour when He will pay for your sins and mine. It is the hour when all the creation of God will see the love of God displayed and lavished as He takes your sins and my sins upon Himself and dies a vicarious, substitutionary, redemptive death for you and for me. And it won't end there; it will go on to the Resurrection.

"The hour is come; glorify thy Son, that thy Son also may glorify thee." The death of Christ will demonstrate that God is not the brutal bully the liberal theologians talk about in the Old Testament, but that He is a loving Father who so loves the world that He gives His only begotten Son. Then the Son will be raised from the dead, ascend back into heaven, and He will be given a name that is above every name, that at the name of Jesus every knee should bow to Him. "Glorify thy Son, that thy Son also may glorify thee." Oh, the wealth of meaning that is here!

> **As thou hast given him power over all flesh, that he should give eternal life to as many as thou hast given him [John 17:2].**

This is a startling statement. He has power over all flesh! He could make this universe and every individual in it bow to Him. He could bring us all into subjection to Him and make robots out of all of us. Although that is the last thing He would want to do, He has the power over all flesh.

The church is God's love gift to Jesus Christ. So He gives eternal life to as many "as thou hast given him." This brings up the question of election and free will, and I don't want to go into that extensively. There are extreme Calvinists and extreme Arminians, and the truth is probably somewhere between the two. If God would somehow reveal to me who are the elect ones, I would give the gospel only to them. But God does not do this. He has said that whosoever will may come. That is a legitimate offer to every person. You have no excuse to offer at all if you will not come to Him. It will be your condemnation that you turned down the offer that God has made to you.

> **And this is life eternal, that they might know thee the only true God, and Jesus Christ, whom thou hast sent [John 17:3].**

Does election shut out certain people? No. Life eternal is to know the only true God and Jesus Christ whom He has sent. Do you have a desire to know the true God and Jesus Christ? Then you are not shut out. You must be one of the elect. He gives eternal life to those who have heard the call and have responded down in their hearts. They have come to Christ of their own free will.

"That they might know thee." It is not the amount of knowledge you have, but the kind of knowledge that is important. It is whom you know. Do you know Jesus Christ? In the same way, it is not the amount of faith you have but the kind of faith that is important. There is a song called "Only Believe." Only believe what? Only believe in the only One, the Lord Jesus Christ. I quote Spurgeon again: "It is not thy joy in Christ that saves thee. It is Christ. It is not thy faith in Christ, though that be the instrument. It is Christ's blood and merit." It is Christ who saves. One can believe in the wrong thing. It is the *object* of faith which is so important. "This is life eternal, that they might know *thee* the only true God, and Jesus Christ." Now faith comes by hearing, hearing the Word of God. What does the Word of God say? The gospel is that Jesus died for our sins, was buried, and rose again. Those are the facts. Our knowledge of the facts and our response to that knowledge is faith. Faith is trusting Christ as our own Savior.

Life eternal is to *know* God and to *know* Jesus Christ. Jesus is His name as Savior, and Christ is His title—the Messiah, the King of Israel. To know Him means to grow in grace and in the knowledge of Christ. When we move on in the knowledge of the Lord Jesus Christ, we come to the place of assurance. Anyone without the assurance of salvation is either unsaved or is just a babe in Christ. They need to move on to the place where they *know* that they are saved. Life eternal is to know the only genuine God and to know Jesus Christ. This is the reason that the study of the Word of God is so important. Many people stay on the fringe of things and are never sure they are saved.

I have glorified thee on the earth: I have finished the work which thou gavest me to do [John 17:4].

The Lord Jesus is handing in His final report to the Father. He hasn't died on the Cross yet; but, as far as God is concerned, He speaks of things which are not as if they are. Future tense for God is just as accurate as past tense. Our Lord Jesus is going to the Cross to die and then will rise again. On the Cross, He said, "It is finished" (John 19:30). That means our redemption was finished. He has done everything that was necessary. We can put a period there. We cannot add a thing to His finished work. Therefore, the gospel of salvation is not what God is asking you to do, but what God is telling you that He has already done for you. It is your response to that which saves you.

> **And now, O Father, glorify thou me with thine own self with the glory which I had with thee before the world was [John 17:5].**

In Philippians 2, it speaks of Jesus emptying Himself. Some try to teach that He emptied Himself of His deity. John makes it very clear that the Word became flesh. That little baby in Mary's lap is God, and He could have spoken this universe out of existence. He wasn't just 99.9% God; He was, and is, 100% God. So of what did He empty Himself? He emptied Himself of His prerogatives of deity; He laid aside His glory.

At Christmas we make a great deal of the shepherds and the angels and the wise men who came to see Him. Friend, that is not the way it should have been. He is the Lord of glory, and the whole creation should have been there; every human being on the face of the earth should have been there. People will come from all parts of a country and even all parts of the world for the funeral of a great political leader. The whole world should have been at the birth of the Lord of glory when He came to earth. Although He could have claimed such homage, instead He laid aside His glory. Now He is ready to return to heaven, back to the glory.

JESUS PRAYS FOR DISCIPLES

> **I have manifested thy name unto the men which thou gavest me out of the world: thine they were, and thou gavest them me; and they have kept thy word [John 17:6].**

Notice this: "to as many as thou hast given him" (v. 2): "unto the men which thou gavest me . . . and thou gavest them me" (v. 6); "for them which thou hast given me" (v. 9); "whom thou hast given me" (v. 11); and "those that thou gavest me" (v. 12). We are back to the great doctrine of election. Jesus talked to the Father about it. It was a private conversation, but He wanted the disciples to hear it and to know about it. I don't know as much about election as maybe I should know. I've read Hodge, Calvin, Thornwall, Shedd, and Strong on the subject, and they don't seem to know much more about it. The reason we know so little about election is because it is God's side, and there are a lot of things that God knows that we don't know.

It is a wonderful thing to be able to listen to this prayer and to know that Jesus is at God's right hand talking to the Father about us. The Lord Jesus has talked to the Father about you today, if you are one of His.

There is a mystical relationship between the Lord Jesus and His own. They belong to the Father and were given to Jesus Christ. I can't fathom its meaning. What a wonderful relationship!

> **Now they have known that all things whatsoever thou hast given me are of thee.**
>
> **For I have given unto them the words which thou gavest me; and they have received them, and have known surely that I came out from thee, and they have believed that thou didst send me [John 17:7–8].**

The Lord had given them the Words of the Father. That is important. He had not given them property or money or an automobile, but the Words of the Father. Jesus testifies here that these disciples believed that He came from the Father. They knew who He was. They did not understand His purpose and certainly not His death and resurrection, but they had made tremendous advances during the three years they had been with Him. They knew He had come from God, and they believed that God had sent Him.

> **I pray for them: I pray not for the world, but for them which thou hast given me; for they are thine [John 17:9].**

I will make a startling statement which is no more startling than what He made: Jesus Christ does not pray for the *world* today. His ministry of intercession is for His own who are in the world. He doesn't pray for the world; He *died* for the world. What more could He do for the world? He has sent the Holy Spirit into the world to convict the world of sin, righteousness, and judgment. Jesus Christ prays for His own.

And all mine are thine, and thine are mine; and I am glorified in them [John 17:10].

The whole purpose of our salvation is to bring glory to Jesus Christ.

And now I am no more in the world, but these are in the world, and I come to thee. Holy Father, keep through thine own name those whom thou hast given me, that they may be one, as we are [John 17:11].

He prays for two wonderful things. He prays for us to be kept. You will be kept because you have been sealed by the Holy Spirit and because your Savior is praying for you.

His other request is that we should be one. He prays for the unity of believers. He's not praying for an ecumenical movement or that we all join the same denomination. There has been much wrong teaching about this. First of all, He prays to the Father that His own might be one. Notice that He isn't praying to us or to some church authority; He is praying to the Father. And He prays that we should be one "as we are"; that is, as the Father and the Son are one. The Father has answered every prayer of His Son, and He has answered this one. There is an organic unity which God has made. The Holy Spirit takes all true believers and baptizes them into the body of Christ, identifies them in the body of Christ. The disgrace of it all is that down here the believers are pretty well divided. But there is only one true church, and every believer in Jesus Christ is a member of that church. It is called the body of Christ.

While I was with them in the world, I kept them in thy name: those that thou gavest me I have kept, and none of them is lost, but the son of perdition; that the scripture might be fulfilled [John 17:12].

"Those that thou gavest me"—we have election mentioned again. There are certain things which I believe that to me are not contradictory, but they certainly are paradoxical. Election and free will happen to be one of those. I wish you could have met me when I graduated from seminary. I was a smart boy then and I even had the answer to election and free will. But I have a little more sense than I had then, and I realize that we simply do not understand it.

Judas Iscariot is, of course, "the son of perdition." He fulfilled the prophecies concerning him.

And now come I to thee; and these things I speak in the world, that they might have my joy fulfilled in themselves [John 17:13].

Friend, God does not want us to be long–faced, solemn Christians. He came that our lives might be filled with joy—His joy.

I have given them thy word; and the world hath hated them, because they are not of the world, even as I am not of the world [John 17:14].

The Word of God causes problems in the world today. The Bible is the most revolutionary Book in the world. It is revolutionary to teach that you cannot save yourself, that only Christ can save you. And you can't make this world better. Only Jesus Christ can do that. That's revolutionary, and the world doesn't want to hear that. They'd rather plant a few flowers and try to clean up pollution. The problem is that the pollution is in the human heart.

I pray not that thou shouldest take them out of the world, but that thou shouldest keep them from the evil [John 17:15].

This really should read "from the evil one." Again it is startling to note that He does not pray that we should be taken out of the world. God gets glory by keeping you and me in the world today. We think of the Rapture as wonderful, and it will be. We think of the Rapture as bringing glory to God, and it will. But let's understand one thing: God gets glory by keeping you and me in the world. If you knew Vernon McGee like He knows Vernon McGee, you'd know it is a miracle for God to keep me in the world. We long for the Rapture. In Revelation 22:17 it says that the Spirit and the bride say, "Come." The Holy Spirit is weary of this world, He is grieved. He says, "Come." We also are weary, and we who are the bride of Christ say, "Come." But Jesus prays not that we should be taken out of the world, but that we should be kept from the evil one, Satan. And I wouldn't want to be here for a minute if my Lord weren't keeping me from the evil one.

Wouldn't it be wonderful if we could really learn this lesson? We cry and whimper because things are hard down here. Sure they are. He said they would be hard—"but be of good cheer; I have overcome the world" (John 16:33). I suspect that every twenty-four hours there is a great hallelujah meeting in heaven, and the angels say, "Isn't it marvelous that McGee is still being kept. It would be so easy to take him out of the world, but it is a real miracle to keep him in the world." If we could learn that, it would enable us to endure more easily our problems and tensions and difficulties and temptations. The Lord Jesus has prayed to keep us in the world and to protect us from the evil one.

They are not of the world, even as I am not of the world [John 17:16].

The measure in which we as believers realize this, the more completely we fulfill His will and accomplish His purpose.

Sanctify them through thy truth: thy word is truth [John 17:17].

Sanctify means to set apart. The believer is not of the world; he is set apart. The thought has reference to the task rather than the person; it is a commitment to the task. The believer is set apart by the Word of God. That is, the Word reveals the mind of God. As you read the Word, you are led to set yourself apart for a particular ministry. We can serve Him only as we know His Word and are obedient to it.

As thou hast sent me into the world, even so have I also sent them into the world.

And for their sakes I sanctify myself, that they also might be sanctified through the truth [John 17:18–19].

We have been sent out into the world to bear a witness. He sets Himself apart to be identified with us, and we ought to be identified with Him in this world.

JESUS PRAYS FOR HIS CHURCH

Neither pray I for these alone, but for them also which shall believe on me through their word [John 17:20].

He had you and me in mind. Now, many centuries later, we can know our great High Priest is praying for us.

That they all may be one; as thou, Father, art in me, and I in thee, that they also may be one in us: that the world may believe that thou hast sent me [John 17:21].

This prayer has been answered. The church is an organic unity. Believers are one in Christ, for the church is one body. The minute any sinner trusts Christ, that sinner is put into the body of Christ. If believers would manifest that union to the world, the world would be more impressed with Christ. Too often the world sees believers hating each other which may well be one of the reasons they will not accept Christ.

> **And the glory which thou gavest me I have given them; that they may be one, even as we are one:**
>
> **I in them, and thou in me, that they may be made perfect in one; and that the world may know that thou hast sent me, and hast loved them, as thou hast loved me [John 17:22–23].**

"I in them, and thou in me." How wonderful! Only the Spirit of God can accomplish that. The unity that exists between the Father and the Son is the unity that is to exist between the believer and the Lord Jesus Christ! "And hast loved them, as thou hast loved me"—means that God loves you as much as He loves the Lord Jesus Christ. That boggles the mind!

> **Father, I will that they also, whom thou hast given me, be with me where I am; that they may behold my glory, which thou hast given me: for thou lovedst me before the foundation of the world [John 17:24].**

It will be heaven to be with Him in perfect fellowship. I take it that this was God's purpose in creating man. There are other creatures in the universe and on the earth, but God made man a creature with whom He could have fellowship. God created man with a free will; and, even though man sinned, God wants his fellowship. Heaven is going to be wonderful, and it will be important that every one of His sheep is there with Him. Each one will have his contribution to make.

To behold the glory of the Lord Jesus will be the satisfaction of the believer. Moses asked to see the glory of God. Philip asked to see the Father. Sometimes we get a glimpse of glory in a rainbow or a sunset.

Think what it will be when we come into His presence and behold His glory! That is the goal to which we are moving.

> **O righteous Father, the world hath not known thee: but I have known thee, and these have known that thou hast sent me [John 17:25].**

Being sent from the Father actually embraces His entire mission of redemption. Anyone who is a believer knows that the Father has sent Him, and the purpose was for Him to die for our sins.

> **And I have declared unto them thy name, and will declare it: that the love wherewith thou hast loved me may be in them, and I in them [John 17:26].**

The last thing He mentions is that His love might be in our hearts and in our lives. We talk so much about grace and about faith, and rightly so; yet the great desire of His heart is that His love should be manifest in the lives of those whom He has redeemed. That should put us down on our faces before Him. My friend, how much of His love is manifest in you?

In review, this is what this prayer says about believers and the world:

1. Given to Christ out of the world (v. 6)
2. Left in the world (v. 11)
3. Not of the world (v. 14)
4. Hated by the world (v. 14)
5. Kept from the evil one (v. 15)
6. Sent into the world (v. 18)
7. Manifest in unity before the world (v. 23)

These are the requests of Christ for His own:

1. Preservation (v. 11)
2. Joy—fullness of the Spirit (v. 13)
3. Deliverance—from evil (v. 15)
4. To be set apart—"sanctify" (v. 17)

5. Unity—"be one"—(this is not union) (v. 21)
6. Fellowship—"be with me" (v. 24)
7. Satisfaction—"behold my glory" (v. 24)

The Lord Jesus Christ is our great High Priest. This is the great truth of the Epistle to the Hebrews. In the Old Testament economy the high priest wore an ephod of beauty and glory, which was joined on each shoulder by two onyx stones with the names of the tribes of Israel engraved on them. Thus he carried the names of the children of Israel with him when he went into the presence of God. This speaks of the strength and power of the high priest. Hebrews 7:25 tells us about Jesus Christ, our High Priest: "Wherefore he is able also to save them to the uttermost that come unto God by him, seeing he ever liveth to make intercession for them." Christ is *able* to save us, you see. He has strength and power.

Also on the breastplate of the high priest were twelve precious stones, arranged three in a row in four rows across his breast. On each was the name of a tribe of Israel. When the high priest went into God's presence wearing the breastplate, he pictured the Lord Jesus Christ who is at the right hand of God interceding for us. The Lord not only carries us on His shoulders, the place of strength and power, but He also carries us on His breast, on His heart, which speaks of His love. He has all power, and He loves us!

CHAPTER 18

THEME: Arrest and trial of Jesus—the arrest in Gethsemane; trial before Annas; first denial by Simon Peter; trial before high priest; second denial by Simon Peter; trial before Pilate

We have now concluded the Upper Room Discourse which began in John 13 and was climaxed with this wonderful prayer of the Lord Jesus in John 17. Augustine made this statement about the discourse: "It is easiest in regards to words but most profound in regards to ideas." That certainly is a true statement.

We come now to the fifth division of this Gospel of John: the witness of Jesus to the world. It includes chapters 18 to 20. We will see in this chapter that He is arrested and taken before the high priest. The presentation here is different from that in the synoptic Gospels (Matthew, Mark, and Luke). The emphasis in those three Gospels is upon the humanity of Christ, His human nature, and upon the sufferings of the Savior. In the first three Gospel records, as He approaches Jerusalem, He says He is going there to die. He mentions His death, His treatment, His abuse in the hand of the Gentiles, and then His bodily resurrection.

In the Gospel of John, the emphasis is upon the deity of the Lord Jesus. He is the God-man in this Gospel, and the emphasis here is upon His glory. In His arrest, His death, His resurrection we will see His glory. Remember how often He stated in His discourse that He was returning to the Father. This is in accord with the emphasis on His glory.

THE ARREST IN GETHSEMANE;
TRIAL BEFORE ANNAS

When Jesus had spoken these words, he went forth with his disciples over the brook Cedron, where was a gar-

**den, into the which he entered, and his disciples [John
18:1].**

In these passages we will find a blending of His majesty and His
meekness. He seems to have spent His nights under the open sky. Why
did He leave Jerusalem and cross the brook Cedron? Apparently He
was accustomed to going there.

**And Judas also, which betrayed him, knew the place:
for Jesus ofttimes resorted thither with his disciples
[John 18:2].**

Luke tells us in chapter 21:37, "And in the day time he was teaching
in the temple; and at night he went out, and abode in the mount that is
called the mount of Olives." And again, Luke 22:39: "And he came
out, and went, as he was wont, to the mount of Olives . . . ." He would
need to cross the brook Cedron.

Our Lord crossed over the brook Cedron after Judas had made his
agreement to betray Him. Perhaps you remember another crossing of
this same brook by one who was betrayed—King David, when his son
Absalom led in a rebellion and Ahithophel, his friend and counsellor,
betrayed him.

As far as we can tell, Jesus never spent a night in the city of Jerusalem, in the walled city. The last week of His life, He went to Bethany
and stayed with His friends. Even on this last night, He left the walled
city to go to the place called the Garden of Gethsemane. He is going to
this quiet place in order to give His enemies an opportunity to take
Him. They wanted to lay hands on Him but, because they were afraid
of the people, they wouldn't dare lay hands on Him in the temple or in
the streets of Jerusalem.

Notice that John does not include the agony in the garden. John
does not record His praying and His extreme suffering. Rather he
speaks of the glory. He is putting the emphasis on the deity of Christ,
whereas the other Gospels emphasize His humanity. You will notice
that Jesus will not resist arrest. He is the Lamb of God who offers no
resistance. ". . . as a sheep before her shearers is dumb, so he openeth

not his mouth" (Isa. 53:7). The dignity of His person at this time is absolutely overwhelming.

Remember in previous incidents, when the enemies of the Lord Jesus tried to close in on Him, He hid Himself. Apparently He could just disappear miraculously. Now, He lays Himself wide open to be taken. This is very important for us to note.

Judas then, having received a band of men and officers from the chief priests and Pharisees, cometh thither with lanterns and torches and weapons [John 18:3].

Luke tells us what He said: ". . . Be ye come out, as against a thief, with swords and staves?" (Luke 22:52). It says that a *band* of men came out. A band is the tenth part of a legion and would consist of approximately five hundred men. Matthew says that a great multitude came with Judas. Why would they come with such a multitude and with swords and clubs? That crowd knew that He had performed miracles, and they thought that, if they would bring along a big enough company of armed men, they could capture Him. Now notice the dignity of our Lord.

Jesus therefore, knowing all things that should come upon him, went forth, and said unto them, Whom seek ye? [John 18:4].

My friend, do you think this is just a poor, weak man who has been trapped by some clever religious rulers and the power of Rome? If He had not yielded Himself, all the weapons those men had would have been absolutely useless and worthless.

They answered him, Jesus of Nazareth. Jesus saith unto them, I am he. And Judas also, which betrayed him, stood with them [John 18:5].

I don't want to pass over this because I wouldn't want you to miss this for anything in the world. They call Him "Jesus of Nazareth." They do not accord Him the dignity that belongs to Him. They refuse to call Him the Christ. Well, it's all right, because Jesus is a name that is above every name. The day is coming when those on earth and even those under the earth, in hell itself, will bow the knee to the name of Jesus. But now, this crowd would not acknowledge Him as the Savior, the Christ, the Son of the living God.

They didn't know Him. The thing that is strange above everything else is that Judas didn't know Him at first. Why didn't Judas know Him? Paul says, "But if our gospel be hid, it is hid to them that are lost: in whom the god of this world hath blinded the minds of them which believe not, lest the light of the glorious gospel of Christ, who is the image of God, should shine unto them" (2 Cor. 4:3–4). We are told that the natural man does not receive the things of the Spirit of God neither can he know them because they are spiritually discerned. I believe that Judas did not know Him because He stood there as the Lord of glory.

As soon then as he had said unto them, I am he, they went backward, and fell to the ground [John 18:6].

"And the Word was made flesh, and dwelt among us, (and we beheld his glory, the glory as of the only begotten of the Father,) full of grace and truth" (John 1:14). Even in this dark hour when He was yielding Himself as the Lamb of God that taketh away the sin of the world, He revealed His deity—and they fell backwards! He revealed to these men that He was absolutely in charge, and they could not arrest Him without His permission. They didn't fall forward to worship Him. They fell backward in fear and in absolute dismay. I think there was utter confusion for a moment there when they fell backward. They are seeing not simply Jesus of Nazareth but the God-man, the Lord of glory.

This fulfills prophecy. "The LORD is my light and my salvation; whom shall I fear? the LORD is the strength of my life; of whom shall I be afraid? When the wicked, even mine enemies and my foes, came upon me to eat up my flesh, they stumbled and fell" (Ps. 27:1–2). This is the God–ward side. Then in Psalm 35:4 we see the man–ward side. "Let them be confounded and put to shame that seek after my soul: let them be turned back and brought to confusion that devise my hurt." Then listen to Psalm 40:14: "Let them be ashamed and confounded together that seek after my soul to destroy it; let them be driven backward and put to shame that wish me evil." What a fulfillment we have here when our Lord for a brief moment reveals His glory to them. They are seeking Jesus of Nazareth. Well, here He is, but He is the Lord of glory.

My friend, whom do you see? Do you know who He is? The unsaved man doesn't know Him. People may even read the Bible and be very religious and very moral and not see that Jesus of Nazareth is the Christ, the Son of the living God.

> Then asked he them again, Whom seek ye? And they said, Jesus of Nazareth.
>
> Jesus answered, I have told you that I am he: if therefore ye seek me, let these go their way:
>
> That the saying might be fulfilled, which he spake, Of them which thou gavest me have I lost none [John 18:7–9].

Notice His dignity. He is in charge of everything. He is even telling them whom to arrest and whom not to arrest. There had been the prophecy that the Shepherd would be taken and the sheep scattered, and Jesus had said that He had lost none. The disciples would not be captured. Isn't it interesting that they weren't? One would think they would have been brought in as witnesses or accomplices, but they were not.

> Then Simon Peter having a sword drew it, and smote the high priest's servant, and cut off his right ear. The servant's name was Malchus [John 18:10].

Why didn't they arrest Simon Peter for this?

Then said Jesus unto Peter, Put up thy sword into the sheath: the cup which my father hath given me, shall I not drink it? [John 18:11].

Dr. Luke tells us that Jesus touched the man's ear and healed him. But why didn't they arrest Peter? Because the Lord Jesus said, "You let these men go." He is in command.

Simon Peter, the poor, ignorant fisherman! He probably was really smarting inside. He had asked the Lord why he couldn't go with Him where He was going. He had said he would lay down his life for the Lord, and he meant it. But the Lord had told him that he didn't know himself, that he would deny his Lord that night. Oh, it's so easy to get Christians to dedicate and rededicate their lives to the Lord. Simon Peter would have come forward at every invitation, and he would have meant it. The problem is that we cannot produce this in our own strength. This was Paul's experience, too. He said that to will was present with him, but he couldn't find how to perform it. It is only the power of the Holy Spirit that can produce the life yielded to Christ. I think Peter was smarting inside and thinking, "I'll show Him that I'll die for Him."

Peter's a good fisherman. He can throw a net expertly, but he makes a sorry swordsman. He got an ear when he meant to get a head. Our Lord tells Peter to put up his sword. Earlier, when Jesus advised them to have swords, it was for their protection, not for His defense. Our Lord is yielding Himself into the hands of His captors. He is getting ready, as He says, to drink the cup which His Father has given Him.

There are several "cups" mentioned in the Scriptures. There is the cup of salvation: "I will take the cup of salvation, and call upon the name of the LORD" (Ps. 116:13). Then there is the cup of consolation: ". . . neither shall men give them the cup of consolation to drink for their father or for their mother" (Jer. 16:7). Also there is the cup of joy: "Thou preparest a table before me in the presence of mine enemies: thou anointest my head with oil; my cup runneth over" (Ps. 23:5). This cup which our Lord was to drink was given Him by the Father. It was a dreadful cup, and Jesus prayed in Gethsemane, ". . . O my

Father, if it be possible, let this cup pass from me . . ." (Matt. 26:39). This is the cup of judgment He bore for us on the Cross. Everyone who turns his back on Jesus Christ must drink that cup of judgment himself. Jesus drank it for us although it was totally repulsive to Him. Remember that He was perfect humanity, absolutely sinless, and yet He drank the hated cup because it was the cup of your sin and my sin. There is still another cup, the cup of judgment which is yet to come on this world. I believe the seven vials or bowls of wrath, which are to be poured upon the wicked as described in Revelation are the fulfillment of this. "Upon the wicked he shall rain snares, fire and brimstone, and an horrible tempest: this shall be the portion of their cup" (Ps. 11:6). This is the cup of his anger. "For thus saith the LORD God of Israel unto me; Take the wine cup of this fury at my hand, and cause all the nations, to whom I send thee, to drink it" (Jer. 25:15).

Notice again what our Lord says to Peter, "Put up thy sword into the sheath: the cup which my Father hath given me, shall I not drink it?" It is not, "He is the judge, and I'm going to drink it by command," but, "Shall I not drink this cup my Father gives me?" There is no willingness higher than that. Let us not get the idea that the Savior did this reluctantly. Hebrews 12:2 says, ". . . who for the joy that was set before him endured the cross, despising the shame, and is set down at the right hand of the throne of God."

> **Then the band and the captain and officers of the Jews took Jesus, and bound him,**
>
> **And led him away to Annas first; for he was father in law to Caiaphas, which was the high priest that same year [John 18:12–13].**

The religious rulers were the ones who had plotted all this. Because they were afraid of the people, our Lord went outside the city to give them the opportunity they needed to arrest Him. He is going forward in His dignity and in His glory. They took Him and bound Him— which wasn't necessary. He is the Lamb slain from the foundation of the world. He is the sheep before the shearers; He will not offer any resistance.

They led Him away to Annas first. Only John gives us that detail, as apparently he was in a position to see something that the others didn't see. Annas had been the high priest and was probably still in the quarters of the palace of the high priest. Secular history testifies to the fact that Annas was one of the most brilliant, one of the most clever, and one of the most satanic of all the high priests. Caiaphas was the one whom the Roman government accepted, but the real head of the religious group was old Annas. I believe that he was the real leader, a politician who knew how to handle Rome. It is my judgment that it was he who plotted the arrest, the trial, and the crucifixion of Jesus. The entire trial was a mockery, and I think Annas was behind it all.

What an injustice has been done to the Jews down through the centuries. They have been blamed for the crime of men like Annas, Caiaphas, and Pilate. I do not take the responsibility for the crimes of Jesse James just because he happened to be an American, do you? Romanism for centuries has called the Jewish people the "Christ-killers," which has been the basis for anti-Semitism in Europe. Yet they are not any more responsible than the Gentiles are. In the final analysis, we all are responsible for His death. He died for the sins of the world. There should be no pointing of the finger at any race or group of people.

Now Caiaphas was he, which gave counsel to the Jews, that it was expedient that one man should die for the people [John 18:14].

I believe John puts this in here to show us that it had already been predetermined that the Lord Jesus was to die. They had already decided that. Old Annas knew how to forge a charge against Jesus to get the death penalty from the Roman authorities. The whole trial was nothing but a mockery.

FIRST DENIAL BY SIMON PETER

And Simon Peter followed Jesus, and so did another disciple: that disciple was known unto the high priest, and

went in with Jesus into the palace of the high priest [John 18:15].

That other disciple was John, obviously. John apparently had an "in" with those in Jerusalem, and this enabled him to get a pass for someone else to come in. I want you to see that John apparently was known in these circles, and for John to go in there was no temptation at all. However, it was fatal for Simon Peter to go in there. He was standing on the outside when John got the permission for him to come into the inner court. I want you to see this little byplay at the palace of Caiaphas.

> **But Peter stood at the door without. Then went out that other disciple, which was known unto the high priest, and spake unto her that kept the door, and brought in Peter [John 18:16].**

John had an entree, but Peter is a poor fisherman whom nobody knows, and he can't get in. John tells the girl at the gate that this is a friend of his, and so he brought Peter in. Simon Peter was scared to death. You see, John was at home here, but Simon Peter had never been in that crowd before. Peter has a big mouth, and he just has to talk. Remember the other Gospels tell us that the girls spot him as a Galilean because his speech betrays him. He talks too much. He's nervous in there. A little wisp of a girl makes him deny the Lord.

There is an application for us here. You and I have no right to put our little ideas of separation down on another Christian. Another Christian may be able to go where you cannot go. It was wrong for Simon Peter to go in there, but it was not wrong for John.

> **Then saith the damsel that kept the door unto Peter, Art not thou also one of this man's disciples? He saith, I am not [John 18:17].**

She knows the followers of Jesus are there and assumes Peter is one of them. She just asks the question as he is about to go through the gate,

"Aren't you one of this man's disciples?" He says, "I am not," and
walks on through.

> And the servants and officers stood there, who had
> made a fire of coals; for it was cold: and they warmed
> themselves: and Peter stood with them, and warmed
> himself [John 18:18].

Outside the palace grounds the people are gathered—not many at that
time of morning, but the guards are there to keep order. They build a
fire, and Peter stands with them warming himself.

TRIAL BEFORE HIGH PRIEST

> The high priest then asked Jesus of his disciples, and of
> his doctrine.

> Jesus answered him, I spake openly to the world; I ever
> taught in the synagogue, and in the temple, whither the
> Jews always resort; and in secret have I said nothing.

> Why askest thou me? ask them which heard me, what I
> have said unto them: behold, they know what I said
> [John 18:19–21].

The scene shifts back to the trial of the Lord Jesus. Notice the dignity
of the Lord Jesus.

> And when he had thus spoken, one of the officers which
> stood by struck Jesus with the palm of his hand, saying,
> Answerest thou the high priest so?

> Jesus answered him, If I have spoken evil, bear witness
> of the evil: but if well, why smitest thou me? [John
> 18:22–23].

He is subject to this kind of humiliation. He is yielding Himself to die
for your sin and my sin. However, He does call their attention to the

fact that what they are doing is illegal and contrary to the Mosaic Law. They have no witness that He has done evil, and yet they smite Him. They are the ones who are breaking the Law. For one thing, no trial is to begin at night nor end at night. A trial is not to begin and end on the same day. They are not to strike a prisoner who has not yet been proven guilty.

Now Annas had sent him bound unto Caiaphas the high priest [John 18:24].

John puts this little verse in to tell us again that it was Annas who bound Him. Annas is the one who plotted and planned all of this diabolical plot.

SECOND DENIAL BY SIMON PETER

And Simon Peter stood and warmed himself. They said therefore unto him, Art not thou also one of his disciples? He denied it, and said, I am not.

One of the servants of the high priest, being his kinsman whose ear Peter cut off, saith, Did not I see thee in the garden with him?

Peter then denied again: and immediately the cock crew [John 18:25–27].

We learn from the other Gospels how Peter went out and wept bitterly. I think that he caught a glimpse of the face of our Lord all bloody and beaten, and he caught His eye. That is when he went out and cried like a baby. You know that if he was arguing with a kinsman of Malchus, he must have been pretty vehement. He denied his Lord. But, thank God, the Lord was on His way to die for him and had already told him that He had prayed so that Peter's faith would not fail.

Why is it that Simon Peter, who did a deed as dastardly as Judas, could make his way back to the Lord? Because he was a child of God, and it broke his heart to know what he had done. A child of God may

get far from God, but God is never far from him. You may be dead to
God, but God is never dead to you. He is always there and He is always
available. The Lord never said to Peter, "I'm sorry, but because you
failed Me, I just can't use you anymore." No, He appeared personally
to Peter after His resurrection, and He elected Peter to preach the first
sermon on the day of Pentecost. There has never been a sermon like it!
Thank God for a Savior and a Lord like that. He will always take you
back!

TRIAL BEFORE PILATE

**Then led they Jesus from Caiaphas unto the hall of judg-
ment: and it was early; and they themselves went not
into the judgment hall, lest they should be defiled; but
that they might eat the passover [John 18:28].**

There is quite an interesting byplay here that I want you to see. Here
we see "religion" and the person of Jesus Christ side by side. Here is
the One who has come to fulfill the Passover. He is going to die on the
Cross because they are bringing the death sentence against Him. But,
because they want to eat the Passover, these men won't go inside the
judgment hall. That would pollute them. They will not do that. Are
they meticulously religious! Yet they are plotting the death of the very
One who is the fulfillment of the Passover! My friend, how this should
cause you to search your heart at this time. Are you merely religious
or are you joined to the Lord Jesus Christ?

There is another interesting byplay to watch here. The Jews absolutely would not go into the judgment hall and thus contaminate
themselves, but they brought Jesus to be taken into the judgment hall
to be tried. Also there is a change of scene in this drama from outside
to inside and inside to outside. Watch it:

"Pilate then went out" (v. 29).

"Then Pilate entered into the judgment hall again" (v. 33).

"And when he had said this, he went out again unto the Jews"
(v. 38).

"Then Pilate therefore took Jesus, and scourged him" (John 19:1).

"Pilate therefore went forth again" (John 19:4).
"And went again into the judgment hall" (John 19:9).
"He brought Jesus forth" (John 19:13).

Pilate didn't really like Jerusalem. He liked Caesarea which is on the seacoast and has a lovely beach, very much like Florida. During the feast, He would leave Caesarea and come up to Jerusalem, bringing his soldiers with him. Since he was the Roman governor, he was responsible for keeping order at this time when the Jews gathered from all over the world. That was the reason he was in Jerusalem at this time.

> **Pilate then went out unto them, and said, What accusation bring ye against this man?**
>
> **They answered and said unto him, If he were not a malefactor, we would not have delivered him up unto thee.**
>
> **Then said Pilate unto them, Take ye him, and judge him according to your law. The Jews therefore said unto him, It is not lawful for us to put any man to death:**
>
> **That the saying of Jesus might be fulfilled, which he spake, signifying what death he should die [John 18:29–32].**

Pilate senses that something is wrong and he tries, as we would say, to get off the hook. He tells them to judge Jesus themselves. He couldn't understand what was taking place. The problem was that they wanted the death penalty and they had to admit that they were no longer the rulers and no longer had the authority to exact the death penalty. It is interesting that these men were forced to admit this after they had so arrogantly stated in John 8:33: "We be Abraham's seed, and were never in bondage to any man."

John tells us that this fulfilled what Jesus had prophesied. He had told the disciples that the Jewish religious rulers would condemn Him to death and would deliver Him to the Gentiles. He had predicted this months earlier; now He was here, being brought to Pilate, the representative of gentile Rome, by the religious rulers who wanted a death sentence. If the Jews had taken Jesus and had put Him to death according to their law, He would have been stoned to death. Read Psalm 22 again and notice whether it is describing a death by stoning or a death by crucifixion. It is obviously crucifixion, with the piercing of the hands and feet and the agonies of hanging on a cross. The only ones who executed by crucifixion were the Romans. Jesus had to be delivered to the Romans to fulfill Old Testament prophecy.

> **Then Pilate entered into the judgment hall again, and called Jesus, and said unto him, Art thou the King of the Jews?**
>
> **Jesus answered him, Sayest thou this thing of thyself, or did others tell it thee of me?**
>
> **Pilate answered, Am I a Jew? Thine own nation and the chief priests have delivered thee unto me: what hast thou done? [John 18:33-35].**

Jesus had appealed to the head of this man, Pilate. He asked him the logical question of where he got his evidence. Pilate sneered at that and said the Jews had brought the accusation. Now Jesus will appeal to this man's heart. Jesus is dealing with him, man to man.

Pilate was dumbfounded. He couldn't believe there was someone claiming to be the king of the Jews and that they would have the audacity to bring such a charge. Pilate is out on a limb and wants to get off. He would like to help Jesus. He is inside the court, alone with Jesus; the Jews are waiting outside because of their scruples about contaminating themselves. Pilate would be happy if Jesus would simply say He is not a king and that would get Pilate off the hook. Who is on trial? Pilate or Jesus?

> **Jesus answered, My kingdom is not of this world: if my kingdom were of this world, then would my servants fight, that I should not be delivered to the Jews: but now is my kingdom not from hence [John 18:36].**

"My kingdom is not of this world." The preposition is the Greek *ek*, meaning "out of." Literally, He said "My kingdom is out of this world." He is not saying that His Kingdom is not going to be on this earth someday, as He is going to rule as King of kings and Lord of lords and ". . . the earth shall be full of the knowledge of the LORD, as the waters cover the sea" (Isa. 11:9). But His Kingdom is not going to be of this world system. It will not be a power structure built on politics. It will not come through worldly measures. Jesus will not be elected King by either the Democrats or the Republicans or by the United Nations. It is not going to be built by war and turmoil and hatred and bitterness. Pilate, himself, was a crooked politician who bought his job and was a puppet of Rome. He hated the Jews, but he was afraid to offend them because he might lose his job. But Jesus will not come to His Kingdom by political maneuvering. Jesus said, "If my kingdom were of this world, then would my servants fight." He was offering no resistance. Peter had tried to defend Him, and Jesus had told him to put his sword in the sheath. He is not building His Kingdom out of the present political system.

Friend, the church cannot build His Kingdom either. The Bible teaches us clearly that in this present age Christ is gathering out a people for His name (see Acts 15:14). These are the *ekklesia* or the called-out ones, the church. They are called out of the world to live *in* the world but not *of* the world. The time will come when the Lord will completely remove the church from the world. Then, when Christ comes in His Kingdom, He will establish it!

> **Pilate therefore said unto him, Art thou a king then? Jesus answered, Thou sayest that I am a king. To this end was I born, and for this cause came I into the world, that I should bear witness unto the truth. Every one that is of the truth heareth my voice [John 18:37].**

Pilate is definitely puzzled at this point. Jesus is still pleading with this man. He tells him that an essential of His Kingdom is truth. Listen to Psalm 45:1–4: ". . . I speak of the things which I have made touching the king: my tongue is the pen of a ready writer. Thou art fairer than the children of men: grace is poured into thy lips: therefore God hath blessed thee for ever. Gird thy sword upon thy thigh, O most mighty, with thy glory and thy majesty. And in thy majesty ride prosperously because of truth and meekness and righteousness. . . ."

> **Pilate saith unto him, What is truth? And when he had said this, he went out again unto the Jews, and saith unto them, I find in him no fault at all [John 18:38].**

Was Pilate a cynic? Was he simply puzzled? He stood in the presence of the Lord Jesus who was and is the Way, the Truth, and the Life. John tells us later in his Gospel that he has written all these things so that we might believe that Jesus is the Christ, the Son of God. Friend, do you ask, "What is truth?" Is He truth to you? Have you faced reality in Him?

Again he took Jesus outside and declared, "I find in him no fault at all!"

> **But ye have a custom, that I should release unto you one at the passover: will ye therefore that I release unto you the King of the Jews? [John 18:39].**

He was trying desperately to escape making a decision. "Let me release Jesus to you, and that will settle it."

> **Then cried they all again, saying, Not this man, but Barabbas. Now Barabbas was a robber [John 18:40].**

Pilate didn't dream that these religious rulers would urge the people to demand that Barabbas be released. The contrast between them was too great. The Bible makes it clear that Pilate was assured that Jesus Christ was an innocent man.

"He knew that for envy they had delivered him" (Matt. 27:18).

". . . I am innocent of the blood of this just person . . ." (Matt. 27:24).

"For he knew that the chief priests had delivered him for envy" (Mark 15:10).

"Pilate therefore, willing to release Jesus, spake again to them" (Luke 23:20).

". . . I have found no cause of death in him . . ." (Luke 23:22).

". . . I find in him no fault at all" (John 18:38).

". . . From thenceforth Pilate sought to release him . . ." (John 19:12).

". . . Pilate, when he was determined to let him go" (Acts 3:13).

In spite of all this, Pilate did not have the courage to release Him.

CHAPTER 19

THEME: Death of Jesus at Golgotha; burial in the tomb of Joseph

In this chapter we will see a great miscarriage of justice. Rome was noted throughout the world for its justice. On every Roman official's desk there was the little figure of the two-faced god, Janus. One face looked forward and the other face looked backward. (It is from this word that we get the name January for the month that looks back to the old year and forward to the new year.) Janus was to remind the judge to look at both sides of the question. Rome ruled the world for nearly one thousand years. When the Romans took over a people, they promised them good roads, law and order, protection, and peace—but life would be under a dictatorship. Rome ruled with an iron hand. In Roman courts the innocent got justice, and the guilty got justice—not mercy, but justice. The interesting thing that makes this such an anomaly is that the trial of Jesus was one of the greatest miscarriages of justice.

DEATH OF JESUS AT GOLGOTHA

Then Pilate therefore took Jesus, and scourged him.

And the soldiers platted a crown of thorns, and put it on his head, and they put on him a purple robe,

And said, Hail, King of the Jews! and they smote him with their hands [John 19:1–3].

If Jesus was innocent, He should have been turned loose. If He was guilty of the charge brought against Him, He should have been crucified. To scourge Jesus was entirely unlawful and wrong. Pilate did it because he thought this would placate the Jews.

The soldiers took this opportunity to have their fun with Him before He was crucified. When it says "they smote him with their hands," it means they played a cruel Roman game with Him. They could mutilate Him and do anything they wished with Him. All the soldiers would show the prisoner their fists. Then they would blindfold the prisoner and all but one would hit him as hard as they could. Then they would remove the blindfold, and if the prisoner was still conscious he was to guess which soldier did not hit him. Obviously, the prisoner could never guess the right one. They would continue this until they had beaten the prisoner to a pulp. I believe that the Lord Jesus was so mutilated that you would not have recognized Him. "As many were astonied at thee; his visage was so marred more than any man, and his form more than the sons of men" (Isa. 52:14).

> Pilate therefore went forth again, and saith unto them, Behold, I bring him forth to you, that ye may know that I find no fault in him.
>
> Then came Jesus forth, wearing the crown of thorns, and the purple robe. And Pilate saith unto them, Behold the man! [John 19:4–5].

Now they come outside again. I think that if you had seen Him then, it would have broken your heart. He had been beaten within an inch of His life. Don't think He looked like the artists picture Him.

"Behold the man!" If you have said only this that Pilate said, you haven't seen Him at all. He is more than a man. He is the Son of God. He is the Savior of the world. John has written these things so that you might believe that Jesus is the Christ, the Son of God, and that believing you might have life in His name.

> When the chief priests therefore and officers saw him, they cried out, saying, Crucify him, crucify him. Pilate saith unto them, Take ye him, and crucify him: for I find no fault in him [John 19:6].

It may have been at this point that Pilate called for the basin of water and washed his hands. The water would clean his hands but could not cleanse the guilt of his heart. The oldest creed of the church states that Jesus was crucified under Pontius Pilate.

> **The Jews answered him, We have a law, and by our law he ought to die, because he made himself the Son of God.**
>
> **When Pilate therefore heard that saying, he was the more afraid;**
>
> **And went again into the judgment hall, and saith unto Jesus, Whence art thou? But Jesus gave him no answer [John 19:7–9].**

Pilate is not satisfied, and so he takes Him inside again to question Him.

> **Then saith Pilate unto him, Speakest thou not unto me? knowest thou not that I have power to crucify thee, and have power to release thee?**
>
> **Jesus answered, Thou couldest have no power at all against me, except it were given thee from above: therefore he that delivered me unto thee hath the greater sin [John 19:10–11].**

There are differences of sin and differences of judgment. Those who delivered Jesus to Pilate had the greater sin because they had more light than Pilate did. However, that does not exonerate Pilate at all. He is guilty.

> **And from thenceforth Pilate sought to release him: but the Jews cried out, saying, If thou let this man go, thou art not Caesar's friend: whosoever maketh himself a king speaketh against Caesar [John 19:12].**

From thenceforth Pilate sought to release Him. Because he believed in Him? No. Because he knew that the Lord Jesus was an innocent man.

Jesus is now in the hands of a cheap politician—not the judge of Roman justice that Pilate should have been. These Jewish religious rulers are prepared to report Pilate to Rome accusing him of permitting subversion. That would be treason, and Pilate doesn't want such a charge against him. Pilate will let his political position overrule his justice. It is a terrible thing, even today, when government, whether it be church or state government, gets into the hands of men who are hungry for power and do not regard either God or man.

> **When Pilate therefore heard that saying, he brought Jesus forth, and sat down in the judgment seat in a place that is called the Pavement, but in the Hebrew, Gabbatha [John 19:13].**

The Pavement was the *Lithostrotos*. It was the place of Roman justice. Julius Caesar always carried a moveable one with him so that anywhere he went, the *Lithostrotos* was set up, and there he pronounced his judgments. This Gabbatha is one place in Jerusalem which I think is accurately identifiable. It is about fifteen feet below the present level of the Ecce Homo Street. There is the worn stone which I think may well be the Pavement, the Gabbatha.

> **And it was the preparation of the passover, and about the sixth hour: and he saith unto the Jews, Behold your King!**
>
> **But they cried out, Away with him, away with him, crucify him. Pilate saith unto them, Shall I crucify your King? The chief priests answered, We have no king but Caesar [John 19:14–15].**

Notice the dignity of the Lord Jesus through all this. Notice that He is not the one on trial. Pilate is forced to a choice. Will it be Jesus Christ or Caesar? The religious leaders are forced to a choice. Will it be Jesus Christ or Caesar? They make their dreadful choice, "We have no king but Caesar." The day will come in the future when they will have to make another choice. Jesus Christ or the Antichrist? Friend, listen; every man must make his choice about Jesus Christ. He says, "He that is not with me is against me . . ." (Matt. 12:30). The minute you make a decision against Christ, you make a decision for "Caesar."

Then delivered he him therefore unto them to be crucified. And they took Jesus, and led him away [John 19:16].

We speak so often of the death and resurrection of Jesus Christ that it becomes almost trite for the average believer. The crucifixion of Jesus Christ is one of the most dastardly, infamous points in history. Yet, this is our redemption. We need to pause here and look at it from various points of view.

From the standpoint of God, the Cross is a propitiation. It is the mercy seat where God can extend mercy to you and to me. It is the place where full satisfaction was made, so that a holy, righteous God can reach down and save sinners. The very throne of God, the place of judgment, is transformed into the place of mercy where you and I can find mercy instead of the judgment we deserve. Jesus Christ bore our guilt, and God is satisfied.

From the standpoint of the Lord Jesus, it is a sacrifice. He is the Savior, and He makes Himself an offering for sin. He is a sweet-smelling savor to God. It is also an act of obedience for Him. Paul tells us in Philippians 2:8 that he became obedient to death, even the death of the cross.

From the standpoint of you and me, believers in Christ Jesus, it was a substitution. He took my place and He took your place. He was the sinless One suffering for the sinner. He was the just One suffering for the unjust. "Who his own self bare our sins in his own body on the tree, that we, being dead to sins, should live unto righteousness: by whose stripes ye were healed" (1 Pet. 2:24).

From the standpoint of Satan, it was a triumph and also a defeat. It was a triumph for Satan to bruise the heel of the woman's seed as had been foretold way back in Genesis 3. It was a defeat because the head of Satan is yet to be crushed: ". . . that through death he might destroy him that had the power of death, that is, the devil" (Heb. 2:14).

From the standpoint of the world, the Cross is nothing but a brutal murder. They see Jesus of Nazareth. They see the man. They see the injustice.

So they led Him away to be crucified. This fulfills Psalm 94:20–21: "Shall the throne of iniquity have fellowship with thee, which frameth mischief by a law? They gather themselves together against the soul of the righteous, and condemn the innocent blood."

> **And he bearing his cross went forth into a place called the place of a skull, which is called in the Hebrew Golgotha:**
>
> **Where they crucified him, and two other with him, on either side one, and Jesus in the midst [John 19:17–18].**

John does not give us a picture of the Crucifixion. He mentions the place but gives very few details. General Gordon, never satisfied with the spot inside the city walls which is pointed out as Golgotha, decided upon a rocky, skull–like formation outside the city walls, called Gordon's Calvary, which I believe to be the actual Golgotha.

You will recall that every bit of the sin offering was taken outside the camp into a clean place (see Lev. 4:12). Just as the Lord Jesus fulfilled prophecy concerning Himself, so He also fulfills the types in the Old Testament. Our sin offering, the Lord Jesus Christ, was taken outside the city. The writer to the Hebrews emphasizes the fact that our Lord suffered outside the gate (see Heb. 13:12).

> **And Pilate wrote a title, and put it on the cross. And the writing was, JESUS OF NAZARETH THE KING OF THE JEWS [John 19:19].**

You will notice that I have made no attempt to harmonize the other Gospels with the Gospel of John. They are each different, and each is written for a different purpose. You need to put all four of them together to find the complete statement written on the Cross.

> **This title then read many of the Jews: for the place where Jesus was crucified was nigh to the city: and it was written in Hebrew, and Greek, and Latin.**
>
> **Then said the chief priests of the Jews to Pilate, Write not, The King of the Jews; but that he said, I am King of the Jews.**
>
> **Pilate answered, What I have written I have written [John 19:20-22].**

It was written in Hebrew, the language of religion. It was written in Greek, the language of culture and education. It was written in Latin, the language of law and order. Thus, it was written for the whole world to see that He died for all. This is the gospel that is to be preached to the world. This is the hope of the world.

> **Then the soldiers, when they had crucified Jesus, took his garments, and made four parts, to every soldier a part; and also his coat: now the coat was without seam, woven from the top throughout.**
>
> **They said therefore among themselves, Let us not rend it, but cast lots for it, whose it shall be: that the scripture might be fulfilled, which saith, They parted my raiment among them, and for my vesture they did cast lots. These things therefore the soldiers did [John 19:23-24].**

"When they had crucified Jesus." No Gospel writer describes the death of Christ. There are things about the Cross and the Crucifixion that are hidden from us. God pulls down a veil on many of the details. Darkness covered the land so the people couldn't see. First of all, God is not going to give us morbid details simply to satisfy our idle curiousity. Secondly, there was a transaction between the Father and the Son taking place there. It was a transaction for the sins of the world, which is beyond our comprehension. The only thing that we can do is to accept by faith the forgiveness that is made ours through Christ's death on the Cross. That is the only way you and I will ever penetrate that darkness, my friend.

Apparently His garment is a peasant's garment but a good one. Someone had made it for Him. The soldiers cast lots for it—shot dice at the foot of the Cross. Although these Romans do not know it, they are fulfilling the Scriptures: "They part my garments among them, and cast lots upon my vesture" (Ps. 22:18).

> **Now there stood by the cross of Jesus his mother, and his mother's sister, Mary the wife of Cleophas, and Mary Magdalene.**
>
> **When Jesus therefore saw his mother, and the disciple standing by, whom he loved, he saith unto his mother, Woman, behold thy son!**
>
> **Then saith he to the disciple, Behold thy mother! And from that hour that disciple took her unto his own home [John 19:25–27].**

Jesus calls Mary, "Woman," just as He had in John 2 at the wedding at Cana. His hour is come. He is to die, but He will rise again. He is to be glorified. His relationship to His mother is to be severed. To her, as well as to us, He is to be the glorified Christ. His resurrection will clear her name forever. Her reputation will be vendicated. But she must come to Christ in faith just as every other believer comes. While He is dying for the sins of the world, He will not neglect her. We know that Mary will be praying with the disciples in the Upper Room after His resurrection (see Acts 1:14), and after that she drops out of the picture. As long as she lived John would keep her in his home and care for her, as the Lord Jesus asked him to do.

After this, Jesus knowing that all things were now accomplished, that the scripture might be fulfilled, saith, I thirst.

Now there was set a vessel full of vinegar: and they filled a sponge with vinegar, and put it upon hyssop, and put it to his mouth.

When Jesus therefore had received the vinegar, he said, It is finished: and he bowed his head, and gave up the ghost [John 19:28–30].

John carefully shows us that scripture is being fulfilled. There are chapters in the Old Testament which are especially concerned with the Crucifixion. I would list Psalm 22, Genesis 22, Isaiah 53, and Leviticus 16. There are twenty–eight prophecies fulfilled while He was hanging on the Cross. "I thirst" is the fulfillment of Psalm 69:21.

"It is finished!" What was finished? Your redemption and my redemption was finished. In His report to the father He had said, "I have finished the work which thou gavest me to do" (John 17:4).

The Jews therefore, because it was the preparation, that the bodies should not remain upon the cross on the sabbath day, (for that sabbath day was an high day,) besought Pilate that their legs might be broken, and that they might be taken away.

Then came the soldiers, and brake the legs of the first, and of the other which was crucified with him.

But when they came to Jesus, and saw that he was dead already, they brake not his legs:

But one of the soldiers with a spear pierced his side, and forthwith came there out blood and water.

And he that saw it bare record, and his record is true: and he knoweth that he saith true, that ye might believe.

> For these things were done, that the scripture should be fulfilled, A bone of him shall not be broken.
>
> And again another scripture saith, They shall look on him whom they pierced [John 19:31–37].

The first prophecy which John mentions was fulfilled. It says "He keepeth all his bones: not one of them is broken" (Ps. 34:20). The second one still awaits fulfillment. ". . . they shall look upon me whom they have pierced, and they shall mourn for him, as one mourneth for his only son . . ." (Zech. 12:10). He has been pierced! That part has been fulfilled. But Zechariah says that He shall return again, and when He comes, then they shall look upon the One whom they have pierced, and they shall mourn for Him.

BURIAL IN THE TOMB OF JOSEPH

We are dealing with facts, the great historical facts of the gospel. What is the gospel? Paul defines it for us. "For I delivered unto you first of all that which I also received, how that Christ died for our sins according to the scriptures; and that he was buried, and that he rose again the third day according to the scriptures" (1 Cor. 15:3–4). These are the central facts of the gospel. Our salvation is based on our relationship to those facts and to the person of Jesus Christ. Do you trust Him? Do you have faith in what He did for you when He died on the Cross? Do you believe that He died a vicarious, substitutionary, redemptive death for you?

> And after this Joseph of Arimathaea, being a disciple of Jesus, but secretly for fear of the Jews, besought Pilate that he might take away the body of Jesus: and Pilate gave him leave. He came therefore, and took the body of Jesus.
>
> And there came also Nicodemus, which at the first came to Jesus by night, and brought a mixture of myrrh and aloes, about an hundred pound weight.

Then took they the body of Jesus, and wound it in linen clothes with the spices, as the manner of the Jews is to bury [John 19:38-40].

The two men who handle the body of Jesus are both prominent men. Joseph of Arimathaea is a rich man, and Nicodemus is the ruler of the Jews who had come to Jesus by night. They were both secret disciples, but now they come out in the open for the first time. Let's not be too critical of these men. They had stayed in the background but, now that the Lord's disciples have all scattered like sheep and gone under cover, these two men come out in the open.

Because the children of Israel had lived in Egypt, some believe that they were the ones who perfected the method of embalming that the Egyptians used. The child of God in the Old Testament as well as the New Testament has always believed that the body will rise again. It is sown in corruption; it will be raised in incorruption. It is sown in weakness; it will be raised in power. It will be a glorified body. For that reason, the child of God has a reverence and a care for the body.

The custom was to use about half the body weight of spices; so we can guess that the Lord Jesus weighed about two hundred pounds. They would prepare the body by rubbing it with myrrh and aloes, then wrapping it with linen strips. That would seal it and keep out the air. They would begin with a finger, then wrap all the fingers that way, then the hand, the arm, and the whole body. In other words, they wrapped the body of the Lord Jesus like a mummy. Now John mentions specifically that they wrapped the body in the linen cloth using the spices, because this is a very important detail for him. You remember that on the resurrection morning, when John saw the linen lying there and the body not in it, he understood that the Resurrection had taken place, and he believed.

Now in the place where he was crucified there was a garden; and in the garden a new sepulchre, wherein was never man yet laid.

There laid they Jesus therefore because of the Jews' preparation day; for the sepulchre was nigh at hand [John 19:41–42].

They had to hurry because of the approaching Passover, and apparently they didn't get the embalming process completely finished. This explains why the women bought more spices and planned to come to care for the body of the Lord after the feast day.

This moves us into the next glorious chapter.

CHAPTER 20

THEME: Resurrection of Jesus; appearance to Mary; appearance to the disciples; appearance to Thomas

This is the resurrection chapter as it is recorded in John's Gospel. The resurrection of Jesus Christ is the very heart–blood of the Christian faith. It is so important that someone has said, "We cannot make too much of the death of Christ, but we can make too little of the resurrection of Christ." That is the thing that is happening today. Theology books, hymns of the church, sermons, all devote sections to the death of Christ. Too often the resurrection of Christ is observed only on Easter. We should note that the sermons in the New Testament, beginning at Pentecost, have the resurrection of Jesus Christ as their theme.

RESURRECTION OF JESUS

The first day of the week cometh Mary Magdalene early, when it was yet dark, unto the sepulchre, and seeth the stone taken away from the sepulchre [John 20:1].

"The first day of the week," that is, Sunday, Mary Magdalene came to the tomb. When was the Sabbath Day changed? This question is often asked by folk who believe we should be observing Saturday as the day of rest and worship. It was changed when Jesus Christ arose from the dead. He was dead during the Sabbath Day; He became alive on Sunday. From that time on, believers have been gathering together on the first day of the week. The Sabbath Day belongs to the old creation. After God had created everything, He rested on the Sabbath Day. Now we have come to the new creation in Christ Jesus. Pentecost occurred on Sunday, the first day of the week. It is interesting that John, the last of the Gospel writers, emphasizes that it was the first day of the week when Jesus rose from the dead.

It will be helpful to get in our minds the order of events on this morning of the Resurrection. I quote from a footnote in *The Scofield Reference Bible*, page 1043.

> Three women, Mary Magdalene, and Mary the mother of James, and Salome, start for the sepulchre, followed by other women bearing spices. The three find the stone rolled away, and Mary Magdalene goes to tell the disciples (Lk. 23:55—24:9; John 20:1-2). Mary, the mother of James and Joses, draws nearer the tomb and sees the angel of the Lord (Mt. 28:2). She goes back to meet the other women following with the spices. Meanwhile Peter and John, warned by Mary Magdalene, arrive, look in, and go away (John 20:3-10). Mary Magdalene returns weeping, sees the two angels and then Jesus (John 20:11-18), and goes as He bade her to tell the disciples. Mary (mother of James and Joses), meanwhile, has met the women with the spices and, returning with them, they see the *two* angels (Lk. 24:4-5; Mk. 16:5). They also receive the angelic message, and, going to seek the disciples, are met by Jesus (Mt. 28:8-10).

Mary Magdalene was the one from whom the Lord had cast seven demons. Some Bible students think she was the sinful woman who wiped the feet of Jesus with her hair. This is an assumption which cannot be proved. I take it that she was a person of very high caliber. She was eternally grateful to the Lord for healing her. When she saw the body was not here, she immediately ran to tell John and Peter.

> **Then she runneth, and cometh to Simon Peter, and to the other disciple, whom Jesus loved, and saith unto them, They have taken away the Lord out of the sepulchre, and we know not where they have laid him [John 20:2].**

The disciple "whom Jesus loved" is John. He always refers to himself in this way rather than by name. Any of the disciples, except Judas, could have used this title for himself. You can use it for yourself. Jude

21 says, "Keep yourselves in the love of God, looking for the mercy of our Lord Jesus Christ unto eternal life." Keep yourself in the love of God, because you know that He loves you. You can't keep Him from loving you! It is wonderful to take that position for yourself as John did: "the other disciple, whom Jesus loved."

We find Simon Peter and John together. Apparently John has taken him in. I wonder if some of the other disciples, when they heard of Peter's denial, had pushed him to the outside. Thank God, John took him in at a time when Peter desperately needed someone to befriend him. John, the son of thunder, has become the apostle of love. What a wonderful thing that is.

Mary Magdalene was not expecting the Resurrection. Her thought was that someone had stolen away the Lord's body. Isn't it interesting that the religious rulers would later accuse the disciples of stealing the Lord's body, and that Mary's first thought was that the religious rulers had stolen the Lord's body? (The religious rulers would have given everything in the world if they could have produced the body on that first Sunday!)

> **Peter therefore went forth, and that other disciple, and came to the sepulchre.**
>
> **So they ran both together: and the other disciple did outrun Peter, and came first to the sepulchre [John 20:3–4].**

Simon Peter and John were not expecting the Resurrection. They probably thought that Mary didn't really see well in the dark. She saw the stone rolled away, became frightened, and ran. Or maybe she went to the wrong tomb. So they rush to the cemetery. Friend, you don't go into a cemetery to look for the living. They were not expecting to look for the living. They were not expecting to find Jesus alive when they rushed to the tomb. They were expecting to find the Lord's body.

This "other disciple" was John. He was a younger man and could outrun Simon Peter. This confirms tradition that John was probably the youngest of the disciples. I am of the opinion that these men represented quite an age span. John may have been in his late teens.

And he stooping down, and looking in, saw the linen clothes lying; yet went he not in [John 20:5].

What John saw convinced him that Jesus had risen from the dead. He got there first, but because he had a certain amount of reticence and reverence, he didn't go in. He stooped down to look in through the very small entrance that was hewn out of the stone. He saw the evidence that convinced him. It is amazing how God uses little things like this to bring conviction to the hearts of men. Someone has said, "Great doors swing on little hinges." John saw the linen cloth lying there, but the body had gone out of it.

Then cometh Simon Peter following him, and went into the sepulchre, and seeth the linen clothes lie [John 20:6].

Then here comes Simon Peter puffing and blowing. I tell you, it was hard on him to run. Reticence is not one of his qualities; so he goes right into the sepulchre. He, too, sees the linen clothes and the wrapping that was around His head. Remember that Joseph and Nicodemus had wrapped our Lord's body in the linen and had sealed it with the myrrh and aloes, which made a sort of glue to seal in the body. How could the body get out of such an encasement without unwinding all that linen?

Jesus Christ came up out of that tomb just like a seed comes out of the soil. Remember He had said that a grain of corn falls to the ground and remains alone unless it dies. Then new corn will grow out of it. But the old shell of the seed is still in the ground. That is what was left in the tomb—just the old shell that He had been in. He was no longer in that shell. He was alive.

Do you remember that when the Lord Jesus raised Lazarus, he came forth from the grave all wrapped in the graveclothes and the Lord had to tell them to loose Lazarus? Lazarus came out in his old body wrapped in the old graveclothes. The body of Lazarus would have to die again. However, Jesus Christ came forth in a glorified body which will never see death. This is the Resurrection!

> **And the napkin, that was about his head, not lying with the linen clothes, but wrapped together in a place by itself.**
>
> **Then went in also that other disciple, which came first to the sepulchre, and he saw, and believed [John 20:7–8].**

God carefully records through John another small but important detail. The napkin that was wrapped around His head lay there intact, separate from the linen wound around His body. It was in the shape of the head, lying just as it had been folded around the head. I think this convinced Peter that the Lord had risen. There are three different Greek words used in this passage, and they are all translated as "seeing." This is unfortunate. In verse 5, when John stooped down, looked in and *saw*, the word means *to perceive and understand*. It involves inspection and perceiving. In verse 6, when Peter went in and *saw*, the word used is *theaomai* from which we get our word *theater*. He viewed it. In verse 8, when John went into the sepulchre and *saw*, it means *to know*. He knew and he believed before he ever saw the risen Christ.

> **For as yet they knew not the scripture, that he must rise again from the dead.**
>
> **Then the disciples went away again unto their own home [John 20:9–10].**

John tells us something strange. These men had not understood even though Jesus had told them repeatedly that He would rise from the dead, and even though the Old Testament spoke of this. Even today we need the New Testament as sort of a flashlight to go back and interpret the Old Testament. I believe that one of the reasons the Old Testament is not popular is because we do not sufficiently use the New Testament to interpret it.

There are a great many of us today who read the Bible but still do not know certain scriptures. I believe there are two reasons for this.

One is that we may read a passage many times and each time see things in the passage that we have never seen before. The Holy Spirit gives us further light as we study and read the passages over and over again. Also I believe that we must experience some of the scriptures to understand their meaning. The trials and sufferings and experiences of life explain their meaning to us. For example, when David wrote that the Lord was his Shepherd, he knew from experience the shepherd-care of God.

APPEARANCE TO MARY

Apparently Mary is the first one to whom the Lord appeared. There are eleven appearances before His ascension and three after His ascension. I think we can surmise from the text that there are others which were not described.

A proverb can be found for all situations. For those who ask why Jesus appeared first to Mary Magdalene, Proverbs 8:17 says: "I love them that love me; and those that seek me early shall find me." She sought Him and she sought Him early.

> **But Mary stood without at the sepulchre weeping: and as she wept, she stooped down, and looked into the sepulchre,**

> **And seeth two angels in white sitting, the one at the head, and the other at the feet, where the body of Jesus had lain.**

> **And they say unto her, Woman, why weepest thou? She saith unto them, Because they have taken away my Lord, and I know not where they have laid him.**

> **And when she had thus said, she turned herself back, and saw Jesus standing, and knew not that it was Jesus.**

> **Jesus saith unto her, Woman, why weepest thou? whom seekest thou? She, supposing him to be the gardener, saith unto him, Sir, if thou have borne him hence, tell**

**me where thou hast laid him, and I will take him away
[John 20:11–15].**

Again we are interested in the fact that she does not know Him. Do
you know why? She does not believe that He is back from the dead.
Unbelief is blind and unbelief is dumb, as in the case of Zacharias.
She loves Him, yes, but love must be coupled with faith. She is weeping because she loves Him but also because she does not believe.

How much is the glorified body changed? I don't know, but I don't
think the change is so great that this accounts for her lack of recognition of Jesus. I believe that Mary is absolutely single-minded in her
grief. Although she sees two angels, this doesn't seem to draw her
attention in any particular way. They ask a question, not because they
don't know the answer, but because they are trying to arouse some
evidence of faith in Mary. She is single-minded in her answer. He is
still dead, and the probable answer is that the body has been stolen, as
Mary reasons it out. She does not expect to see Christ alive; and, in
her unbelief, she does not recognize Him.

**Jesus saith unto her, Mary. She turned herself, and saith
unto him, Rabboni; which is to say, Master [John 20:16].**

When He called her by name, she recognized the voice as only He
could speak. I am of the opinion that if the Lord should tarry and all of
us go through the doorway of death, our bodies will be raised when
He calls us by name someday, just as He called by name those whom
He raised from the dead over nineteen hundred years ago.

**Jesus saith unto her, Touch me not; for I am not yet as-
cended to my Father: but go to my brethren, and say
unto them, I ascend unto my Father, and your Father;
and to my God, and your God [John 20:17].**

The Lord told Mary not to touch Him. The word *touch* is *haptomai*,
meaning "to hold on." Later, He told the disciples to touch Him. Why
this difference? He says to her, "for I am not yet ascended to my

Father." This is the reason she should not hold on to Him. So apparently He did ascend to His Father before the appearance to the disciples in the house. I believe that the Lord Jesus presented His blood at the throne of God and that His blood turned the judgment seat into the mercy seat which it is today. That blood was shed for your sin and for my sin. I think the blood will be there throughout all eternity as an eternal testimony of the price He paid for us.

You will notice He was specific in calling God "my Father, and your Father; and to my God, and your God." His relationship to the Father is different from our relationship to Him. We become the sons of God through faith in Jesus Christ, while Christ is a member of the Trinity, the eternal Son of God. He made this distinction here.

APPEARANCE TO THE DISCIPLES

Mary Magdalene came and told the disciples that she had seen the Lord, and that he had spoken these things unto her.

Then the same day at evening, being the first day of the week, when the doors were shut where the disciples were assembled for fear of the Jews, came Jesus and stood in the midst, and saith unto them, Peace be unto you [John 20:18–19].

This group of men had scattered when He was crucified, but now, apparently, had regathered and were hidden away in a room because they were frightened. The doors were shut, which actually means they were locked.

Have you noticed that when the supernatural touches the natural the message is always "Peace" or "Fear not"? His word to them now, when His deity touches their humanity, is "Peace." This is the peace that comes from being justified by faith through our Lord Jesus Christ, which gives us peace with God.

Here, you see, they knew Him when they saw Him. These men

were frightened, of course. He appeared in His glorified body and came into the room even though the doors were locked. We learn from this that the glorified body is not subject to the laws of the material universe. That is why I believe that when the Rapture occurs and our bodies are changed, there will be no problem for us to meet the Lord in the air.

> **And when he had so said, he shewed unto them his hands and his side. Then were the disciples glad, when they saw the Lord [John 20:20].**

Notice, that even though He has a glorified body, there are the nail prints and the pierced side. There is a strange similarity to that body which had been nailed to the Cross. The scars are there. Now I do not think that there will be scars on our bodies. I think these scars are on His body because they are the scars He bore for us. He was scarred for us so that you and I might be presented without spot or blemish before Him. He took our sin and this will be the evidence of it throughout eternity.

> **Then said Jesus to them again, Peace be unto you: as my Father hath sent me, even so send I you [John 20:21].**

I do not think the Lord is just repeating Himself. I think this is a different peace here. In verse 19, it was the peace of redemption—peace *with* God. Redemption is now complete. This is the peace described in Matthew 11:28: "Come unto me, all ye that labour and are heavy laden, and I will give you rest." This is the rest of redemption, the peace of redemption.

There is another peace. It is the peace of those who are in fellowship with God and are doing His will. This is the peace described in Matthew 11:29: "Take my yoke upon you, and learn of me; for I am meek and lowly in heart: and ye shall find rest unto your souls."

Redemption is now accomplished. Now Christ sends them out as the Father had sent Him into the world. He had previously mentioned this in His prayer, "As thou hast sent me into the world, even so have I also sent them into the world" (John 17:18).

And when he had said this, he breathed on them, and saith unto them, Receive ye the Holy Ghost [John 20:22].

This period of history is a transition period between law and grace. There is an interval in the life of these men and in the ministry of the Lord Jesus between His death and resurrection and the Day of Pentecost. This is a time unique in the history of the world.

Our Lord had told them about prayer back in Luke 11. He had said that if they would ask, it should be given to them. In verse 13 of that chapter, He says that He is speaking especially of the gift of the Holy Spirit which the heavenly Father would give to them who ask Him. Well, as nearly as we can tell they never asked! In John 14:16 Jesus says, "And I will pray the Father, and he shall give you another Comforter." It is true that Simon Peter showed some discernment when he said that Jesus is the Christ, but it was just a few minutes later that he told Jesus not to go to the Cross to die. I personally believe that at the moment our Lord breathed on them, and said, "Receive ye the Holy Ghost," these men were regenerated. Before this, they had not been indwelt by the Spirit of God.

This expression "breathed on them" occurs only one other time in the Bible. In Genesis, God breathed into Adam the breath of life. I believe here that Jesus Christ breathed into these men eternal life by giving them the Spirit of God. This would sustain them and secure them for the interval between His ascension and the coming of the Holy Spirit on Pentecost.

On the Day of Pentecost, the Holy Spirit would come and they would be baptized by the Spirit into the body of Christ. Also they would be indued with power from on high. The church would come into existence on that day. From that time to the present, the Holy Spirit is in the world. He indwells the believer, and He baptizes every believer into the body of Christ.

Whose soever sins ye remit, they are remitted unto them; and whose soever sins ye retain, they are retained [John 20:23].

This is an important verse which is greatly misunderstood. John Calvin writes: "When Christ enjoins the apostles to forgive sins, He does not convey to them what is peculiar to Himself. It belongs to Him to forgive sins. He only enjoins them in His name to proclaim the forgiveness of sins."

Nowhere in the Book of Acts or in the Epistles do we find any instance of an apostle remitting the sins of anyone. They do go everywhere, proclaiming the forgiveness of sins. Let me ask the question: What is it that forgives sins? Even God cannot just arbitrarily forgive sins. Forgiveness of sins is only and alone through the blood of Jesus Christ. Back in the Old Testament, the forgiveness of sins was based on the fact that Christ would come and die. God saved "on credit" in the Old Testament until Christ would come and pay the penalty. Today God forgives our sins when we believe that Christ died for them.

How can you and I remit sins? By telling the gospel! This is the greater work which we shall do. When somebody turned and believed on Jesus while He was here on earth, that was wonderful. But what is staggering is when you or I simply give out the Word of God, and someone is born again and becomes a new creature in Christ Jesus. "Whose soever sins ye remit, they are remitted unto them" happens when you and I proclaim the gospel of the grace of God. That is the most glorious privilege that there is today, my friend.

We have a responsibility. If we do not preach the gospel to the world, their sins will not be remitted. I think we are reaping the penalty for the years we have not taken the gospel to the world. Because we have neglected our responsibility, our boys die in war. Just think, if all the boys we have lost in war had been willing to lose their lives for Christ and be missionaries, how different the world might be! We have the only thing that will bring forgiveness to the world. It is the gospel of Jesus Christ. My friend, what are you doing?

APPEARANCE TO THOMAS

But Thomas, one of the twelve, called Didymus, was not with them when Jesus came [John 20:24].

I can only surmise why Thomas was not there. I think he was a lone wolf and a doubter. He would cast gloom on every situation. I believe the other ten disciples were excitedly talking about Jesus being raised from the dead and Thomas just couldn't believe it.

The other disciples therefore said unto him, We have seen the Lord. But he said unto them, Except I shall see in his hands the print of the nails, and put my finger into the print of the nails, and thrust my hand into his side, I will not believe [John 20:25].

Boy, is he a doubter! He has enough evidence to make him a believer, but he is not. But at least now it appears that he will stay with the other disciples.

My friend, if you are going to grow in grace, you will have to come together with the saints and grow with them. I believe you have to share what you learn from the Word of the Lord. "Not forsaking the assembling of ourselves together, as the manner of some is; but exhorting one another: and so much the more, as ye see the day approaching" (Heb. 10:25). We are to come together so we may grow together.

And after eight days again his disciples were within, and Thomas with them: then came Jesus, the doors being shut, and stood in the midst, and said, Peace be unto you.

Then saith he to Thomas, Reach hither thy finger, and behold my hands; and reach hither thy hand, and thrust it into my side: and be not faithless, but believing.

And Thomas answered and said unto him, My Lord and my God [John 20:26-28].

The record doesn't tell us that he ever reached forth his hand to touch Him. He didn't have to. I know that today there are many people who say, "If only I could see Him, if only I could touch Him, then I would believe." The problem is not with the lack of available evidence of the death and Resurrection. The problem is in the human heart.

God will meet the honest doubt of a man, but I do not think He deals with dishonest doubts. Many people say they can't believe the Bible. They claim their problem is intellectual. Friend, most people will not believe the Bible because of moral problems. A man told me just the other day that he couldn't believe the Old Testament. Later I learned that he is living in adultery. The Old Testament says "Thou shalt not commit adultery" (Exod. 20:14). He doesn't want to believe the Old Testament. However, I am confident that God will always meet an honest doubter.

You will never find a higher testimony to the Lord Jesus than the one given by Thomas. It is one of the great confessions of Scripture. For a Jew to say "My Lord and my God" is the absolute climax. This comes from the lips of that doubter, Thomas.

Jesus saith unto him, Thomas, because thou hast seen me, thou hast believed: blessed are they that have not seen, and yet have believed [John 20:29].

There is a special blessing on us today who believe the evidence for the death and resurrection of Christ.

And many other signs truly did Jesus in the presence of his disciples, which are not written in this book:

But these are written, that ye might believe that Jesus is the Christ, the Son of God; and that believing ye might have life through his name [John 20:30-31].

This is the key to the gospel. The Lord did many things that are not recorded. He healed multitudes. I think John also means that He did many other things after His resurrection which are not recorded. John has been selective in his writing of this Gospel. He has chosen the material which he has written because he had a definite purpose in mind.

John did not attempt to write a biography of Jesus Christ. He did not even attempt to fill in the life of Christ in areas not covered by the other Gospels. He wrote so that you might "believe that Jesus is the Christ, the Son of God; and that believing ye might have life through his name." It is through believing that you receive life and are born again. You become a child of God through faith in the Lord Jesus Christ.

CHAPTER 21

THEME: Epilogue—Glorification; the resurrected Jesus is still God; Lord of our wills—Directs our service; Lord of our hearts—Motive for service; Lord of our minds—Lack of knowledge no excuse from service

Chapter 21 is an epilogue. I believe that after John had written his Gospel, he added the prologue and the epilogue.

There are three incidents in this chapter. There is the fishing experience on the Sea of Galilee (also called the Sea of Tiberias). It shows the Lord Jesus as the Lord of our wills, and He directs our service. The second incident is the breakfast on the seashore. This shows the Lord Jesus as the Lord of our hearts and presents our love for Him as the motive for service. The third incident is Jesus announcing the death of Simon Peter. It shows the Lord Jesus as the Lord of our minds and teaches that lack of knowledge or variation of circumstance is no excuse from service. The entire chapter reveals to us that the resurrected Jesus is still God.

LORD OF OUR WILLS—DIRECTS OUR SERVICE

After these things Jesus shewed himself again to the disciples at the sea of Tiberias; and on this wise shewed he himself.

There were together Simon Peter, and Thomas called Didymus and Nathanael of Cana in Galilee, and the sons of Zebedee, and two other of his disciples.

Simon Peter saith unto them, I go a-fishing. They say unto him, We also go with thee. They went forth, and entered into a ship immediately; and that night they caught nothing [John 21:1–3].

This little Sea of Galilee is so much connected with the ministry of our Lord both before and after His resurrection. It is a familiar spot for these men. He had asked them to go up into Galilee and there He would meet them. They have gone there, and they are waiting for Him.

This is an amazing group here. I like to call this the convention of the problem children. Here is Simon Peter, fervent but failing, warmhearted, yet walking afar off; he is impulsive and impetuous and affectionate. Then here is Thomas, that magnificent skeptic, who has a question mark for a brain; Nathanael, the wisecracker, who was also a doubter at the beginning; the sons of thunder, James and John; and two others who are not named. Perhaps, since this is a crowd of problem children, they represent you and me.

Many worthy commentators condemn these men for going fishing. Well, the Lord did not rebuke them when He appeared to them. They were at Galilee by His commandment. It was springtime, the Passover season. Warm zephyrs from the south made ripples near the shore and whitecaps out on the sea. The surrounding hills were green, and there were wild flowers in profusion. I saw it like that a few days after Easter several years ago, and I imagine it was even more beautiful nineteen hundred years ago. They may have waited and waited for the Lord Jesus to come. Peter would be the one to become impatient, and after pacing back and forth and after looking up and down the shore, would be the one to say, "I go a-fishing." And six others joined him.

They fished all night and caught nothing. This may be the only true fish story that has been told! Dr. Scotts calls it the failure of the experts. Now these men fished all night, and they caught nothing. They had been restless before, and now they are restless and frustrated. It's easy to fish when you catch fish and frustrating when you don't. They knew how to fish—that's the way they made their living—but that night of failure was in the plan and purpose of God for them.

Then morning dawned, and it must have been a glorious morning on the Sea of Galilee. On the morning I was there, I just felt like shouting when I thought of this incident.

But when the morning was now come, Jesus stood on the shore: but the disciples knew not that it was Jesus [John 21:4].

I think this was a normal experience. He was in His glorified body and He could be recognized; yet they would have been a distance out on the lake, and in the early morning it would be difficult to identify people on the shore.

Then Jesus saith unto them, Children, have ye any meat? They answered him, No [John 21:5].

The word for children is almost like saying, "Sirs." It is not a term of endearment like "Little children" in 1 John. Their answer is a short "No." It's amazing how emphatic one can be and how little one likes to talk about failure. They answer Him, but they don't want to talk about it. If they had caught any fish, they all would have been showing Him how long they were.

This is a question He is bound to ask every one of us someday: "Did you catch anything? What did you do for men down there on earth?" I hope your answer will not be the same as theirs, "No, we haven't caught a thing."

And he said unto them, Cast the net on the right side of the ship, and ye shall find. They cast therefore, and now they were not able to draw it for the multitude of fishes [John 21:6].

The whole thought here is that He directs the lives of His own. He gives the instructions, and they are to be obeyed. When they fish according to His instruction, the net fills. Notice the net does not break even though it is full. The net is strong—as strong as the gospel of the death, burial, and resurrection of Christ, of which they are witnesses.

Therefore that disciple whom Jesus loved saith unto Peter, It is the Lord. Now when Simon Peter heard that it

> **was the Lord, he girt his fisher's coat unto him, (for he was naked,) and did cast himself into the sea [John 21:7].**

John has a spiritual perception that Simon Peter doesn't have. Three years before, Jesus had called them at perhaps the same spot. They had gone back to fishing and the Lord had called them again to fish for the souls of men.

Peter may not have the discernment of John, but have you noticed that at every opportunity he gets close to the Lord? The other men sit in the boat and wait until they get to shore. Not Simon Peter. He can't wait. He wants to be close to his Lord. This man is a wonderful man.

> **And the other disciples came in a little ship; (for they were not far from land, but as it were two hundred cubits,) dragging the net with fishes.**
>
> **As soon then as they were come to land, they saw a fire of coals there, and fish laid thereon, and bread.**
>
> **Jesus saith unto them, Bring of the fish which ye have now caught.**
>
> **Simon Peter went up, and drew the net to land full of great fishes, an hundred and fifty and three: and for all there were so many, yet was not the net broken [John 21:8–11].**

This is the last recorded miracle of our Lord, and the only miracle recorded after His resurrection. This is most important because you and I are concerned about the ministry of Christ after His resurrection. Paul says, ". . . yea, though we have known Christ after the flesh, yet now henceforth know we him no more" (2 Cor. 5:16). We are not joined to the baby in Bethlehem but to a resurrected, living, glorified Christ at God's right hand. This is why His ministry after His resurrection is so vital for us.

There are several things I would like to call to your attention here. Have you noticed that the Lord uses what people have as the basis for His miracles? The disciples are fishing and catch nothing. The Lord

Jesus gives them a harvest of fish. At Cana the water pots were empty. The Lord has the pots filled with water and then changes the water to wine. He asks Moses what he has in his hand. Moses says it is a rod, and with that rod, God performs His miracles for Israel. David is faithful as a shepherd with his shepherd's crook, and God gives him a sceptre to hold in his hand. It is interesting that whatever is in your hand, God can use. So many people wish they were somewhere else or in some other circumstances. My friend, if God can't use you right where you are, I don't think He can use you somewhere else.

Besides, have you ever noticed that what God does He does in abundance? The water pots were *full* of wine. There were baskets of food *left over* after the 5,000 had been fed. The nets were *filled* with fish.

Also, notice that although Jesus had fish laid on a bed of coals for their breakfast on the shore of Galilee, He also asks for some of the fish which they had caught. He accepts their service. When they had fished at His command, He accepts what they bring. What blessed fellowship there is in this kind of service!

There was another time when Peter caught a miraculous number of fish, recorded by Luke. It was in the early days of Jesus' ministry, and He was calling Peter to be a fisher of men. That time the net broke. I think Peter was to see that many would follow Jesus, but they would not all be believers. The net would break and many fish would swim away. This time the net did not break but was drawn to land, "full of great fishes." Peter is being called to feed the sheep and feed the lambs. With what? With the Word of God. With the gospel of a risen, glorified Christ. The gospel will not only save, but it will hold. Even in their failures, believers are kept by the power of God through faith.

We see in this incident that Jesus Christ has a purpose for His own. He wants to direct our lives. If we obey, He will bless and have wonderful fellowship with us. He is the Lord of our wills.

LORD OF OUR HEARTS—MOTIVE FOR SERVICE

Jesus saith unto them, Come and dine. And none of the disciples durst ask him, Who art thou? knowing that it was the Lord.

> Jesus then cometh, and taketh bread, and giveth them,
> and fish likewise.
>
> This is now the third time that Jesus shewed himself to
> his disciples, after that he was risen from the dead [John
> 21:12–14].

"Come and dine"—what an invitation! Jesus did say, "Go into all the world and preach the gospel" (see Mark 16:15), but He would rather you would come and have breakfast with Him before you go. The lovely part is that the resurrected Lord, God Himself, feeds them. If only we would sit today and let Him feed us! He wants to feed His own.

Now we come to the special interview that He had with Simon Peter.

> So when they had dined, Jesus saith to Simon Peter, Si-
> mon, son of Jonas, lovest thou me more than these? He
> saith unto him, Yea, Lord; thou knowest that I love thee.
> He saith unto him, Feed my lambs.
>
> He saith to him again the second time, Simon, son of
> Jonas, lovest thou me? He saith unto him, Yea, Lord;
> thou knowest that I love thee. He saith unto him, Feed
> my sheep.
>
> He saith unto him the third time, Simon, son of Jonas,
> lovest thou me? Peter was grieved because he said unto
> him the third time, Lovest thou me? And he said unto
> him, Lord, thou knowest all things; thou knowest that I
> love thee. Jesus saith unto him, Feed my sheep [John
> 21:15–17].

Our Lord takes Simon Peter and calls this faltering, failing, fumbling disciple to service. We learn one all-important lesson from this interview. Love for the Savior is the prerequisite for service.

Three times our Lord interrogates Simon Peter, and three times he responds. Then we find that three times the Lord Jesus Christ gives him his commission.

Why three times? Dr. Godet suggests that the reason lies in the fact that Simon Peter denied Christ three times, and now He makes him affirm his devotion three times. No doubt that is part of the reason, but there is more.

It is quite interesting to note that Simon Peter, with the other disciples, had been called to the ministry—actually had been called into the apostleship—after a miraculous catch of fish. If you will recall the account of this fishing experience back in the Gospels of Mark and Luke you will refresh your mind in the fact that it was after our Lord took over the directing of their fishing that the nets broke—and after that He made them apostles.

Then you will further recall that Simon Peter lost his commission around a little fire of coals that had been built in the courtyard of the palace of the high priest the night Jesus was arrested. Simon Peter went blundering in there to warm his hands and made the fatal mistake of his life. It was there he denied the Lord three times. He should not have gone there, but he did; and when he did, he committed this base denial.

Is it not an interesting thing that now by the Sea of Galilee, around coals of fire, after a miraculous catch of fish, the Lord Jesus restores his commission to him? Here the Lord puts Simon Peter back into service. What a picture of spiritual beauty!

When our Lord asked Peter the question three times, it looks like repetition, but it is not. While there is a similarity in the questions, no two are identical.

The *first interrogation:* "So when they had dined, Jesus saith to Simon Peter [would that we could read this as our Lord said it that morning!], Simon, son of Jonas, lovest thou me more than these?" There are many who express the desire to have had the privilege of being present at certain great occasions in the life of our Lord—when He performed miracles, etc. Candidly, I am not sure that I would want to go back to that day. However, if I could go back and hear Him speak to Simon Peter by the Sea of Galilee, I would go back gladly.

To begin with, He called him Simon. That is interesting—"Simon, son of Jonas." Why did He call him Simon? You will recall when the Lord Jesus first met this man—Andrew brought him to Jesus. When Jesus beheld him, He said (in effect), "Thou art Simon, son of Jonas, thou shalt be called Cephas, which by interpretation is a stone." Cephas is the Aramaic word for "rock man"; in Greek it is Petros. And that name clung to him. We find that over in Caesarea Philippi, when he gave that marvelous testimony concerning the Lord Jesus Christ and said, "Thou art that Christ, the Son of the living God" (John 6:69), the Lord Jesus said in effect, "Blessed art thou, Simon [He goes back to his old name], you will be called Peter because you are going to be a rock man from here on. You will be a man who will stand for something, but right now there is still a question." And so the Lord reminds him of his old name.

There are three words in the Greek language that are translated into the English by the one word love. Perhaps, my friend, you are not aware of the fact that the English language is a beggar for words. We have the one word love and that is about all. You cannot think of another word. Hollywood, today, would give a million dollars for another word. The best they have done is sex and that is pretty low. But the Greek language is a language that is versatile; it is flexible. They have three words for this thing called love.

The first word they have is the word eros. In the use of this word they degraded the meaning of love. The Greeks degraded the word in this use for they personified it. The fact of the matter is they have made "Eros" a god and put together in combination the names Aphrodite and Eros. Today we know these names better as Venus and Cupid. The latter are the Roman names but they are the same, as the Greeks are the ones who started this idea with Aphrodite and Eros. Eros is a word of sensuality and we do believe that the Hollywood word sex, that has really been put into high gear today, would best express what the Greeks had in mind. But this word eros is never used in the Word of God.

There is another Greek word—it is phileō, and it means "friendship." It has to do with the affections and the emotions in human relations at its very best usage. We get our word philanthropic from it, and *philadelphia* comes from it—Philadelphia, the city of "brotherly love." And that is a word that is used in Scripture.

But there is yet another word for love. It is *agapaō. Agapaō* is actually the highest and noblest word for love. Dr. Vincent in his *Word Studies* calls it a word of dignity. It is also a divine word, in that it is a word used to speak of the love of God. The Lord Jesus Christ, in His choice of language, passed over the words *eros* and *phileō* and used the word *agapaō* when He was speaking to Simon Peter. He said, "Do you, Simon Peter, love me with all your heart?"

It is wonderful to have the right doctrine and the right creed, but salvation is a love affair. If you do not love Him, there is no affair. "Simon, son of Jonas, lovest thou me more than these?" Love is the supreme word.

Candidly, if it had been left to me I would have chosen *faith* as the supreme word of Christianity. In fact, I would consider *faith* as the supreme word of any religion. But, of course, Scripture answers that right away: "And now abideth faith, hope, charity [love], these three; but the greatest of these is charity [love]" (1 Cor. 13:13). But I'll tell you why I would choose *faith*—it is a greater compliment to be trusted than to be loved. You see, there is many an old rascal today who is being loved by some wonderful girl. Yes, there is. Sometimes it is the other way around also. But, you see, the minute the object proves unworthy, he is no longer trusted. Will you think closely with me for a minute? Simon Peter had failed the Lord. Actually, the Lord could no longer have confidence in him, but He loved him. Oh, how He loved him!

"Greater love hath no man than this, that a man lay down his life for his friends" (John 15:13). While Simon Peter was denying the Lord, the Lord Jesus was on His way to the Cross to die for him! Later, Peter wrote in his first epistle, "Who his own self bare our sins in his own body on the tree, that we, being dead to sins, should live unto righteousness: by whose stripes ye were healed" (1 Pet. 2:24).

Now notice that our Lord's first question to Peter is, "Lovest thou me more than these?"

What He is saying is: "Do you love Me more than these men love me?" You will recall that the Lord Jesus said, the last time they were in the Upper Room, "One of you will deny Me"—Simon doubtless thought, "Yes, I haven't trusted this crowd either. But there is one fellow here upon whom you can depend—you can depend on me." The Lord Jesus said, "Simon, son of Jonas, are you prepared now to say that you love me more than these other disciples love Me?" That is what He is saying. Now listen to Simon Peter, "Yea, Lord; thou knowest that I love thee." Here Simon came down and would not use the word *agapaō*; he used the word *phileō*. He says, "You know that I have an affection for You."

Why did not Simon Peter use the word our Lord uses? If you want my opinion, this man is through boasting. Never again will he brag of what he will do. Never again will you hear him saying, I am going to do something big for the Lord. For here on he is going to do something big, but he is not going to say anything about it. He comes to the low plain: "I have an affection for You."

Now will you notice the exhortation. Our Lord responds, "Feed my lambs." Let me give you a better translation: "Be grazing my baby lambs"—the word for lambs is diminutive, which means little baby lambs. "Simon Peter, if you love Me I want you to go and graze the little baby lambs; I want you to feed them." Many Christians seem to think He said, "Be criticizing My little lambs." But He has not given you that commission, friend. He says feed them.

The *second interrogation*: Will you notice verse 16, "He saith to him again the second time, Simon, son of Jonas, lovest thou me? He saith unto him, Yea, Lord; thou knowest that I love thee. He saith unto him, Feed my sheep." This time our Lord leaves off "more than these." The reason I think He does it is that He is saying, "Maybe, Simon Peter, you cannot boast anymore and say that you love Me more than do the other disciples, but can you not now say that you do love Me?" In this He is helping this man, trying to lift him up to a higher plane. But Simon Peter just cannot. And somehow we admire him for it. We are glad that he is not boasting anymore. Instead he is willing to take a lower position. Listen to his *affirmation*: "Yes, Lord; thou knowest that I have an affection for thee." But he does not attempt to rise higher—he does not dare to do this, for he is afraid to make such a gesture.

The *second exhortation:* Will you notice this second exhortation, which, incidentally, is ours also. "Feed my sheep." Actually it is not that at all, but rather, "Shepherd the sheep"—that is the word that is used. We want you to notice something, and this is interesting: He says, "feed" the little baby lambs but "shepherd or discipline" the sheep. In our day we have this truth in reverse; we want to discipline the young—that is our method, and we feel as if we should "teach" the old folk. My friend, that is not His method. We are to feed the lambs and shepherd or discipline the older sheep. Do you know why? It is because the little lambs follow the sheep, hence the older sheep must be disciplined.

The *third interrogation:* "He saith unto him the third time, Simon, son of Jonas, lovest thou me?" Christ now adopts the word of Simon Peter when He asks, "Simon Peter, do you really have an *affection* for Me?" Our translation does not show it, but our Lord comes down to the statement of Simon Peter here, and Peter is grieved now.

In the *third affirmation*—"Peter was grieved because he said unto him the third time, Lovest thou me? And he said unto him, Lord thou knowest all things; thou knowest that I love thee."

Let us get at the real meaning of this conversation between our Lord and Simon Peter. Peter was grieved, not because the Lord had asked him the question three times, but he was grieved in his heart because the Lord had to come down and stoop to his level in using his word.

But Simon Peter is still not prepared to climb up. He as much as says that the best thing he can do is to say to the Lord that he has an affection for Him and that the Lord knows he has this affection. He is not bragging now for he realizes that the Lord knows his heart—that he has a real affection in his heart for Him.

The *third exhortation* is "Feed my sheep"—here it has the meaning "be grazing my sheep." You see, the sheep need feeding also.

Milton suffered the loss of a friend, a young minister, who was drowned in the Irish Channel, in crossing; and Milton wrote a poem entitled "Lycidas," in which he made this statement: "The hungry sheep look up and are not fed." In this line he was referring to the pulpit in his day—he might well have been writing of a future day which is ours.

Let me impress it upon your heart that the acid test of any man today, either in pulpit or pew, is "Lovest thou me?"

LORD OF OUR MINDS—LACK OF KNOWLEDGE NO EXCUSE FROM SERVICE

Verily, verily, I say unto thee, When thou wast young, thou girdest thyself, and walkedst whither thou wouldest: but when thou shalt be old, thou shalt stretch forth thy hands, and another shall gird thee, and carry thee whither thou wouldest not.

This spake he, signifying by what death he should glorify God [John 21:18–19a].

Jesus is telling Peter that he is to become a martyr. Peter had said he would lay down his life for the Lord Jesus. Well, that is what he will do.

And when he had spoken this, he saith unto him, Follow me.

Then Peter, turning about, seeth the disciple whom Jesus loved following; which also leaned on his breast at supper, and said, Lord, which is he that betrayeth thee?

Peter seeing him saith to Jesus, Lord, and what shall this man do? [John 21:19b–21].

Isn't this just like this fellow, Simon Peter? He says, "Now you have told me what I am going to do; tell me what John is going to do."

Jesus saith unto him, If I will that he tarry till I come, what is that to thee? follow thou me [John 21:22].

Our Lord is saying, "Look, Simon Peter, you are going to die for me. What John does is none of your business. Even if he lives until I return, that does not affect what you are to do. You follow *Me!*"

> **Then went this saying abroad among the brethren, that that disciple should not die: yet Jesus said not unto him, He shall not die; but, If I will that he tarry till I come, what is that to thee?**

> **This is the disciple which testifieth of these things, and wrote these things: and we know that his testimony is true [John 21:23–24].**

Here is something interesting. Ignorance, or lack of knowledge, is no excuse for not serving the Lord. Some people say they will not serve the Lord if they cannot get all their questions answered. My friend, there are a lot of things that you won't know. There are many things that you don't need to know. There are things that are not your business to know. The important thing is to follow *Him*.

Jesus did not reveal what would happen to John. He simply said that if it were His will for John not to die, that did not affect Peter's service or Peter's obligation to follow Jesus. That is all important for us to see.

Peter wrote in 2 Peter 1:14: "Knowing that shortly I must put off this my tabernacle, even as our Lord Jesus Christ hath shewed me." Tradition says that he was crucified, but that he asked to be crucified with his head down because he was not worthy to be crucified with his head up, as his Lord had been crucified.

My friend, the Lord Jesus Christ must be the Lord of your mind, the Lord of your heart, and the Lord of your will. If He is not the Lord of all, then He cannot be the Lord of your life.

> **And there are also many other things which Jesus did, the which, if they should be written every one, I suppose that even the world itself could not contain the books that should be written. Amen [John 21:25].**

John is not exaggerating when he says the whole world could not hold the books about Him if it all could be written. The Lord Jesus is the One who died on the Cross and rose again from the dead. He is the eternal God, our Savior.

BIBLIOGRAPHY

(Recommended for Further Study)

Gaebelein, Arno C. *The Gospel of John*. Neptune, New Jersey: Loizeaux Brothers, 1925. (Fine exposition.)

Harrison, Everett F. *John: The Gospel of Faith*. Chicago, Illinois: Moody Press, 1962. (A survey.)

Hendriksen, William. *Gospel of John*. Grand Rapids, Michigan: Baker Book House, 1954.

Ironside, H. A. *Addresses on the Gospel of John*. Neptune, New Jersey: Loizeaux Brothers, 1942.

Kelly, William. *An Exposition of the Gospel of John*. Oak Park, Illinois: Bible Truth Publishers, 1898.

Kent, Homer A., Jr. *Fight in the Darkness: Studies in the Gospel of John*. Grand Rapids, Michigan: Baker Book House, 1975. (Excellent for personal or group study.)

Meyer, F. B. *The Gospel of John*. Fort Washington, Pennsylvania: Christian Literature Crusade, n.d. (Devotional.)

Morgan, G. Campbell. *The Gospel According to John*. Old Tappan, New Jersey: Fleming H. Revell Company, n.d.

Pentecost, J. Dwight. *The Parables of our Lord*. Grand Rapids, Michigan: Zondervan Publishing House, 1982.

Pentecost, J. Dwight. *The Words and Works of Jesus Christ*. Grand Rapids, Michigan: Zondervan Publishing House, 1981.

Pink, Arthur W. *The Gospel of John*. Grand Rapids, Michigan: Zondervan Publishing House, 1945. (Comprehensive.)

Robertson, A. T. *Epochs in the Life of the Apostle John*. Grand Rapids, Michigan: Baker Book House, 1935.

Ryle, J. C. *Expository Thoughts on the Gospels,* 4 vols. Grand Rapids, Michigan: Baker Book House, n.d.

Scroggie, W. Graham. *The Gospel of John.* Grand Rapids, Michigan: Zondervan Publishing House, n.d. (Good outlines.)

Tenney, Merrill C. *John: The Gospel of Belief.* Grand Rapids, Michigan: Wm. B. Eerdmans Publishing Co., 1948.

Van Ryn, August. *Meditations in John.* Neptune, New Jersey: Loizeaux Brothers, n.d.

Vine, W. E. *John: His Record of Christ.* Grand Rapids, Michigan: Zondervan Publishing House, 1948.

Vos, Howard F. *Beginnings in the Life of Christ.* Chicago, Illinois: Moody Press, 1975. (Excellent, inexpensive survey.)